YES TO SEX
(JUST NOT YET!)

a practical guide to
sexual integrity
for young adults

SAM BECKWORTH

reaching forward
MEDIA

REACHING FORWARD MEDIA
Yes to Sex... Just Not Yet!
Copyright © 2013 by Sam Beckworth

Requests for information should be addressed to:

REACHING FORWARD MEDIA
email@reachingforwardmedia.com
www.reachingforwardmedia.com

Library of Congress Cataloging-in-Publication Data
Beckworth, Sam
Yes to Sex... Just Not Yet! a practical guide
to sexual integrity for young adults / Sam Beckworth

Cover Design by Dwelling Productions
Printed in the United States of America

ISBN: 0988817608
ISBN-13: 9780988817609

Library of Congress Control Number: 2012923687
Reaching Forward Media, Clovis, CA

Praise for

Yes to Sex... Just Not Yet!

from Singles and Ministry Leaders

Every teenager and young adult should read **Yes to Sex.** *In our culture, where sexuality and sexual morality have been all but obliterated, Sam Beckworth communicates Biblical Truth in a culturally relevant, humorous and logical manner. After reading this book I believe that many teenagers and young adults will begin to understand that the Bible doesn't exist to stifle their fun, but to enrich and deepen their lives and their relationships, as well as to protect them from the consequences of their own poor choices. Although written with teenagers and young adults in mind, I believe that every parent and youth worker should read this book as well. I can think of no better tool to help us to communicate the importance of sexual purity to the young people in our sphere of influence.*

– **Bob Willis**, Lead Pastor,
Northpark Community Church,
Fresno, CA

Pastor Sam did a great job of explaining why waiting for sex is worth it. I enjoyed this book! It's very funny, easy to understand and doesn't make you feel uncomfortable. It has lots of valuable information. Every teen and young adult should read it!

– Olivia De La Cruz, age 14,
Porterville, CA

As a 33-year-old woman waiting for God's best mate for me, this book greatly encouraged me that my commitment to sexual purity is going to lead to a blessed marriage and life. Through personal stories and the Word of God, Pastor Sam rips the seductive mask off of sexual perversion, exposing its true destructive intent for its victims. In a world devastated by compromise, sexual purity is possible and it does matter! Yes to Sex is a challenging and refreshingly honest book that every young person waiting for a godly marriage needs to read.

– Pastor Nicole Avila,
San Jose, CA

As a 24-year-old fresh out of college, I guess you could say I've gone through some temptations in search of the "right one." Pastor Sam's book not only offers great insight on how to live a godly life while being single, but also how to change your spiritual life from the inside out. Not many people can tackle a subject like this with humor and intellect as he does. Although the road ahead isn't easy, I feel more determined than ever to take on this monster called lust. While I've personally struggled in several areas, this book spoke truth concerning my value and that God truly does have a purpose for me. I don't have to live in constant shame. This book is an excellent read for young adults worried about the future and struggling to keep a pure life. Sam makes it clear that my value is found in God alone, and it is He alone I should seek to prepare myself for the one He has for me in the future!

– Mitchell Robinson, age 24,
Newport Beach, CA

My wife and I have had numerous conversations as a result of reading this book. We both wish we had a book like this earlier on in life. We began our marriage later in life and can attest to the truths that Pastor Sam brings to light. He is anointed to bring this vital message to a generation that desperately needs to hear that purity is possible, even in the over-sexualized world we're a part of.

– Paul and Kimberly Haroutunian, M. Div., B.A.
Co-facilitator, Central Valley Youth Ministries
Network, Fresno, CA

In this book Sam shares an easy-to-read, easy-to-understand view of sex as God made it — a good and holy act designed for marriage. He touches on the topics and the scripture that young people need in order to understand God's design, and intention, for sex. One of the few gifts we can bring to God is our obedience; Sam provides tools to help young men and women do just that in the area of sexuality. It will be a volume that will help many young people on their journey.

– Ed Kaczmarek, Executive Director,
Youth For Christ,
Fresno/Madera, CA

Yes to Sex... Just Not Yet! *was a pleasure to read. The combination of humor and scripture brought a fresh take to the idea behind Biblical principles in the sexual world. This book shows young people that God is not someone who desires for the human race to suffer as celibate people for the rest of our lives. It reveals that walking in the perfect divinity of God allows us as human beings to enjoy the splendors that were intended for a certain time in each of our lives.*

– Emily Fernandez, age 20,
Rocklin, CA

Sam's book is a breath of fresh air! Too many books on sexuality for young adults are shaming or guilt-inducing. This message is absolutely pro-sex. It is healthy, encouraging and biblical. It encourages young people to stand up to the lie that "everyone is doing it"; and to those who have failed, it points the way to healing. If you are looking for a guide to navigate the twenty-first century minefield of sexual temptation and arrive whole to stand in front of your future husband or wife, this volume is just what you need.

– Russell Willingham, author of Breaking Free:
Understanding Sexual Addiction and the
Healing Power of Jesus, Director,
New Creation Ministries, Fresno, CA

I really enjoyed how Sam was able to keep the point of the book serious, but also put in small bits of humor. It really did open my eyes. I was able to understand and realize that sex really isn't something you need to be in a hurry for. It takes the right amount of patience and trust in God that what He has planned for you isn't going to be all for nothing, but quite the opposite. Another thing I really enjoyed in the book was the short prayers written at the end of each chapter. I have the final prayer of chapter 12 saved in my notes on my phone. For me personally, I have a totally new and refreshed outlook on the whole sex idea. I know that if I'm just patient with God that He will reward me for putting my trust in Him.

– Christian Lopez, age 14,
Hacienda Heights, CA

Yes to Sex *is a biblical, practical and relevant book that will teach and equip you from the Word of God how to pursue and maintain sexual integrity. Written in a humorous and conversational tone, you will be entertained as you discover the truth about sex. If you're a young adult, this book is written with love and wisdom to you and for you.*

– Pastor John Reeve, M.A Th.,
The Movement Youth Ministry,
The Cause Community Church, Brea, CA

Some ideas that stand out from this book to me are that sex is good and it is meant by God to be enjoyed. There is also a right time for this gift. Quite simply, it pays to wait. Sam's book not only advocates this point, but makes you believe it yourself, and makes you want to live it.

– Chet Frantzich, age 25,
Clovis, CA

Yes to Sex... Just Not Yet! is an insightful, entertaining and prophetic look at one of the most important issues our current generation is facing: sexual purity among believers. With amazing clarity, candor, humor and compassion, Pastor Sam Beckworth delivers a practical handbook for surviving and thriving as a single Christian in an age of tremendous temptations and confusion. This timely book will encourage you, help you and inspire you in your pursuit of sexual wholeness and victory.

– David Cannistraci, Ph.D.,
Lead Pastor, Gateway City Church,
San Jose, CA

Healing, encouragement and a good dose of humor: this book is exactly what Jesus has ordered for this generation. I have been privileged to mentor and lead many young women. Knowing that this book is available for young people looking for a "real life" way of beginning a journey of purity is awesome! To those that are reading this book looking for something different than the empty promises of this world or the disconnected advice from family or friends—know that what is in this book will not condemn you, but encourage and motivate you to get God's best for you! It's time to let go of the lies that have held you in confusion and be free, knowing that sex is good, just not yet!

– Mrs. Elena Robles, Teen Mania's Honor Academy,
Core Advisor Graduate, Clovis, CA

In a world where "anytime sex" is being promoted to people everywhere, Pastor Sam brings the truth about sex and the hope of why we should wait until marriage.

— **Ron "Pup" Nelson**, Fellowship of Christian
Athletes, Central Valley Area Director, CA

This is a fun read. Sam is insightful, humorous, practical and devoid of guilt trips. It's an easy read, loaded with simple wisdom tips for a great life and a future marriage, and what to do if you've done it all wrong!

— **Rick Godwin**, Sr. Pastor/Founder, Summit
Christian Center, San Antonio, TX

This book was not only encouraging in the way of viewing sex as holy, but also in believing that God has a specific person for me. It has been hard to believe that "my person" is still out there. I am now 28, and as that is not old, it can be frustrating trying to be patient for the plans of love and marriage that God has for my life. This book has encouraged me to keep holding on to the promises that God has given me in my future husband and to keep living in a way that is pleasing to God. This book is full of hope. The humor and personal stories makes the subject of sex feel holy and not sinful, when acted upon in God's timing. At no time during reading it did I feel condemned or lectured. I think this book will reach those who have thus far been unreachable because of the condemning nature of other schools of thought out there.

— **Cynthia Schendel**, Dinuba, CA

I'm amazed to see the wonderful gifts of the Lord at work in Sam. His ability to convey wisdom and biblical truth in his first book is one of many ways that God will use him in the future. Pastor Sam is an anointed communicator in teaching and preaching God's Word. I'm very proud to call him pastor, teacher and my son-in-law, my Samuel-son.

— **Mike Rose**, Father-in-Law, Clovis, CA

YES TO SEX
(JUST NOT YET!)

Contents

Dedication   *xiii*

Acknowledgements   *xv*

Foreword   *xvii*

Introduction   *xxi*

Chapter 1   God and Sex:
      Original Intent   *1*

Chapter 2   No Cleavage "Till You Leave-age":
      God's Great Expectations: Be Holy   *7*

Chapter 3   Why Wait to Have Sex?
      A Great Question!   *13*

Chapter 4   What Happens in Vegas Doesn't Stay in Vegas:
      Sexual Sin Runs Deep   *25*

Chapter 5   High Places and Strongholds:
      Everybody Ain't Doing It   *35*

Chapter 6   Restoring Innocence:
      What to Do if You're Already a Mess   *51*

Chapter 7   Resisting Sexual Sin - **Part One**:
             Practical: *Think Mc Fly, Think!*   67

Chapter 8   Resisting Sexual Sin - **Part Two**:
             Spiritual: *Weapons and Armor*   83

Chapter 9   To My Brother from Another Mother:
             What a Guy Wants   121

Chapter 10 To My Sister from Another Mister:
             A Special Message for the Girls   141

Chapter 11 Preparing for "The Right One":
             Letting God Build Your Dream for Marriage   157

Chapter 12 A Word to the Presently Engaged:
             Finish Your Race Well   171

Chapter 13 Speaking to the Gay Sex Issue:
             Gaining a Christlike Perspective   181

Dedication

To the love of my life, Kim: You always make it about me. Perhaps you take better care of me than I do of you. You put me first in every way. I know that I'm blessed and the fear of God helps me to keep in remembrance how good I have it with you. Besides God, your personal encouragement is my greatest fuel. My heart's cry is to cherish and love you as a daughter of the King should be. I am blessed to have you and it is no secret that I married up. Thank you for being my gift, the wife of my youth, and my best friend. Thanks for your belief in me and this book. Obviously, I wouldn't have written it if it wasn't for you. By the way, thank God it's done, right? It seemed like it took forever!

On a more book-appropriate note, thanks for letting me make up for all the times I didn't have sex with you before marriage. I haven't quite caught up but I'm sure in another 30 years or so the numbers will begin to even out. Let's always be busy and stay busy getting busy. I will always and only be "intoxicated with your love." It's still *yes to sex* for you and me! Love you!

Acknowledgements

To Faith Summit Church: You are the most loyal, trusting and loving people any two could pastor. Thank you for supporting, cheering, praying for and believing in us. Love you! Thanks Randy and Julia for your special prayers and prophetic encouragement to get this book started and completed.

To the special people who financially supported this book: you know who you are. Thank you. You have no idea how much your faith in this project meant. May this book bless many in this generation and may God reward you for it!

Thanks to my brother Paul Beckworth and also to Kim Haroutunian for the help with editing. What a blessing and a lot of work for you! Thanks to Jeremy Hendrickson from Dwelling Productions for your design work on the cover, input and editing on the interior, including overall vision for this project. I don't want anyone to know how many hours you donated towards this book. Did I just write that? Much appreciation Jeremy! Thanks also to all of you who pre-read the book, including your honest assessments and kind compliments. I sure appreciated your time I so willingly took from you! Thanks again and God bless.

My father-in-law, Mike Rose: You sacrificed everything for your family. I do not yet understand how a father can invest his whole life into his daughter, only to hand her off to a young man that gets to walk off with her at the altar for free! Thanks for letting me do that with your daughter. She's my greatest gift from God. If I can do half the job you did with my two daughters, I would be considered a great success and a world class father.

My father is my hero. Dad, thanks for paying the raw and ugly price to be the spiritual pioneer in your family. Your sacrifice became my generational blessing. David said, *"One generation shall praise Your works to another."* You made this passage a reality in our lives and it is now being transferred to my two daughters. What a great gift! You and Mom deserve the best. Thanks for being married for nearly fifty years. What a great testimony. Love you Dad and thanks again!

Foreword
by J. Lee Grady

I spend a lot of time encouraging men and women to break free from sexual addictions. At a men's conference I sponsored in 2012 in Philadelphia, some of my friends took the stage and got gut-level honest about their temptations. I was so proud of their courage. Shay, a young father from Ohio, admitted that he was exposed to hard-core pornography when he was only five years old. He began modeling what he saw in X-rated videos when he was just six.

Another guy from Pennsylvania told the men in the audience that he began watching porn when he was a preteen—and this led him to sex with dozens of girls in high school. Until recently this man still battled the shame of his porn habit even though he was a lay leader in his church.

Jason, a youth pastor, preached to the men about how to reclaim purity in our sex-saturated culture. Like so many of the guys in our conference, Jason had been exposed to porn at a young age. His lust could not be satisfied by masturbation or kinkier videos, so his addiction drove him to seek out multiple girls for instant gratification. That's where porn leads.

Meanwhile, at a women's conference I sponsored a few months later, my wife and other friends prayed for a woman who had been raped by a boyfriend. She had never told anyone about her shameful experience, and she didn't know how to break free from the slimy feeling of guilt that had paralyzed her. In the same meeting, we prayed for women who had undergone abortions because they lowered their guard and ended up in bed with guys they hardly knew. We also learned that young women today have been pulled into pornography—not just explicit videos but erotic books like *50 Shades of Gray*. Women today are becoming slaves to sexual immorality.

Thankfully all the people we prayed for in these conferences eventually discovered the grace to escape the trap of sexual sin. Many of them are happily married today, and they've been freed from the shame of past failures. But I meet many Christians who are not so fortunate. A huge percentage of young people in church have given up trying to resist sexual temptation.

If you are one of those men or women who wears a fake smile when you go to church, pretending to be an "overcomer" when you really are a prisoner of lust, then please read this book. Then read it again. Read it three times if you still feel weak!

I am so thankful for my friend Sam Beckworth, who has spent so much time and effort writing this book for you. I believe it is one of the best resources available today on the subject of sexual temptation. Sam is very open about his own life, and he's not afraid to be blunt about a topic that many of our parents were afraid to talk to us about.

After you have read this book, please remember to take these important steps to secure total freedom:

1. Spill your guts. The first step toward repentance is honesty, and it must be brutal. To repent means to turn 180 degrees, so this decision cannot be half-hearted. It's not enough to whisper a quiet prayer under your breath. To break free from a life-controlling habit as powerful as lust, you must talk to someone else. And you should do it sooner, not later.

James 5:16 says, "Confess your sins to one another, and pray for one another so that you may be healed" (NASB). I have prayed with many guys about their pornography addictions, and they have testified that the power of their sin broke the moment they admitted it. Sit down with someone (preferably a more mature Christian you know and trust) and put all your cards on the table. If you humble yourself, God will give you grace to change.

2. Get ruthless. Sin is deceitful. It loves to make up excuses such as, "No one knows about your habit, so it's not hurting anyone," "I deserve this little treat" or "I can play with fire and not get burned." Don't believe the lies. Esau sold his birthright for a bowl of soup, and many people today forfeit their relationship with God by compromising with sexual sin.

You can't break free from a sexual habit by slowly backing away from it or taming it like a pet. The Bible tells us to "flee" from immorality (2 Tim. 2:22). You must lay the axe to the root of your problem. Cut off all access to porn or other forms of temptation. Say goodbye and slam the door in its face. And if you can't stop looking at it on your phone or computer, get rid of your phone and computer!

3. Keep no secrets. Guys with sexual addictions usually struggle with constant shame. They can't enjoy prayer or worship because they feel condemned. They can't share their faith with others because they feel like hypocrites. And many Christians are so full of guilt they turn to alcohol or drugs to numb their pain.

It's not enough to confess your sin once. You must stay in relationship with people who love you enough to confront you. Find one or two accountability partners and make a covenant with them to live transparently. And don't wait until you fall to call for counsel. Contact them whenever you feel tempted. Send up a flare and ask for help before it's too late.

4. Refocus your life on others. Lust is ultimately about self-gratification. When a young man gets hooked on porn, he can't grow up emotionally. This is why some adult men in their 50s and 60s act like 13-year-olds when it comes to sex. They are stuck in perpetual puberty.

You will never break free from the bondage of sexual sin simply by gritting your teeth and trying to forget the images. You must totally redirect your energies toward serving others: your spouse, your children, your church and the needy people around you. Throw yourself into selfless ministry and starve your illegal urges.

5. Stay filled with the Spirit. None of these previous steps are possible without the Holy Spirit, who is our promised Helper (see John 14:16). Self-help is not the answer. Ask the Spirit to fill your life with His refining fire. He will go to the root of your unholy desires, burn up your lust and give you supernatural ability to resist temptation.

J. Lee Grady
Director, The Mordecai Project
Author, *10 Lies Men Believe*

YES to SEX
(JUST NOT YET!)

Introduction

As a young adult you have a lot to deal with. I realize you already know that but perhaps it's appreciated when someone identifies with the tough world you live in. There aren't too many people these days that want to be in your shoes. Between the challenges of school and thoughts of the future, looking for a real friend, family drama and still, after all that, endeavoring to enter adulthood with some framework of character and fear of God, your life can probably get overwhelming. Let's not even touch the larger than life issues like trying to find out who you are or fitting in. I do not want to make you feel any more insecure than you might feel already or predict a grim report about your future. I just think it's important to recognize your life for what it is. You have a huge future ahead of you in God but you also face a legitimate uphill climb to reach it. Simply put, your life demands courage.

With that said, it is quite possible that sexual integrity isn't necessarily a fight you will choose to take on. Christian or not, it may seem easier to live sexually active and not bother swimming against the current of sexual acceptance or even deal with the peer pressure of resisting. Your thoughts might be: *"There are bigger things intimidating me right now and I'm not sure if I have the energy or vision to fight off this battle. I'll just let whatever happens happen—and pay the price later and hope for God's mercy. Maybe He can help me fix whatever problems I might create now through sexual activity later after I'm married."* I don't condemn you for thinking that way sometimes. Besides, you're probably one of the many young adults who loves God and wants to do what's right. If you could snap your fingers and remain sexually inactive until you marry the right one I'm sure you would. Although it doesn't work that way, perhaps if you at least had some helpful tools and enough inspiration, you would probably give Biblical sexual purity a real shot. Well, I believe that God has a message for you to hear and my hope is that some of those helpful tools will be found in this book.

Several years ago the Lord impressed something on my heart about young adults and sex. These were His words as I believe I heard them, "*I want to get My information to them about sex before the world, the flesh and the devil gives their information to them.*" Although that might seem impossible, know for certain that God has a lot of good things to say to you concerning sex and your future spouse. In fact, although it may be hard to believe, God knows how to speak your language. God truly values the distinct cry of your heart and desires to answer you in a way that you can understand and through which you can feel validated. God loves you. He wants you to personally know He respects you and that He identifies with your life on every level. The Lord is not forty galaxies away from you. He is very near to you, wants to bless you and have the bragging rights on your life. I know you want that, too.

Obviously the message I believe the Lord wants to share with you in this book has to do with sex and both the excitement and vision of marrying the person He set aside for you. My hope is that after reading this book you would be encouraged and choose to fight the battle for your sexual integrity. My prayer is that you would see God's heart for you and catch His vision for this huge part of your destiny. Maybe then it would become your passionate desire to pursue His will and experience His best for your life. *Yes to Sex... Just Not Yet!* is part of that plan. On an even higher level this book has to do with inviting the One who is worthy to receive a greater place of worship and rulership in your heart.

The content you are about to read is pretty straightforward and clear. Yes, God commands us to stay away from all forms of sexual immorality and yet He also commands His blessing on our lives. With those two things in mind I encourage you to do your best not to feel condemned or intimidated by any part of this book, especially if you haven't lived a sexually perfect life. We can beat ourselves up pretty good for our own mistakes so we don't need any extra help. At the same time I don't want you to limit your ability, nor the ability of God in you, to live holy before God in your generation. You were created to soar. Get back up if you've stumbled. Dream big and take on the challenge to live above the present culture of sexual compromise. Embrace the grace of God to both live in His mercy, if you mess up, and in His power to live the high life in Christ. You were not created to be enslaved to anything or anyone except for the One who died and now lives to make you free in every way.

Sexual integrity according to the Bible is not about perfectionism. Just as easily as Christians can get sloppy and loose in this area, the best of us, on the flip side, can get legalistic and critical. We won't do well in either extreme. God simply wants your whole heart. God loves and wants the real you, both when you're at your best, and when you're at your worst. He wants you to welcome Him in every part of your life, including that part of you concerning sex, relationships and future marriage. God sees your desire to please Him and your passion to reach for Him in this area. You wouldn't be reading this book right now if it weren't true.

Again, God's will is your sexual purity; but thankfully His way is always best. His instructions are for our benefit. His heart is for our good. Therefore this God-journey is intended to bless you. May this book be fuel for your specific and adventurous journey. I hope you laugh a lot. I hope you feel the love of God. I pray you would, with God's help, be healed from any sexual sin, compromise or rejection you may have already encountered. I pray God would introduce Himself to you in a great and new way. If there's just one thing in this book that speaks to your life and adds value to you, then it's worth it. I would be honored to have been a part of your life in that way.

You are special to God. Your desire for sex and marriage is God-given. He understands you and is bringing you into a place of significance and fulfillment. May you get and stay on His course for your life. Hold on for His best. It's worth any short term sacrifice.

"*For we are God's [own] handiwork (His workmanship), recreated in Christ Jesus, [born anew] that we may do those good works which God predestined (planned beforehand) for us [taking paths which He prepared ahead of time], that we should walk in them [living the good life which He prearranged and made ready for us to live].*" (Ephesians 2:10, AMP)

God bless and enjoy.

Your brother and comrade in battle,

Sam

Chapter 1

God and Sex
Original Intent

Let me start by saying clearly that sex is God's idea and you are absolutely in His will for wanting to have it. God invented sex. God designed sex. God created sex. Nothing is wrong with you for thinking about sex. Actually, much is right with you. You should be looking forward to marriage for the sole purpose of having sex. Genesis chapters one and two could easily say in so many words, "*In the beginning God created sex and saw that it was, indeed, very good.*"

Sex is your gift from God and it is imperative that you hear and believe that sex is good in the mind of God. He's not shy, uncomfortable or insecure about it. He's not mad about it. He's not unclear, silent or unsure about it. He's not intimidated by it. So what's the problem? Well, the challenge is not on His side. Rather, God and sex are both greatly misunderstood, even among Christians. Although this is unfortunate, this reality truly needs to be challenged and changed, especially in the minds of young adults. We're beginning a great journey right now so let's get started.

Negativity Surrounding the Sex Topic

Sex is a dirty word to many Christian young people. At a minimum, the sex topic in the minds of most upcoming adolescents is shrouded with mystery and pre-conceived negativity. This was the case with me back in the fourth grade. For some reason I had this idea that babies were conceived "naturally." I thought a woman just conceived whenever the timing was right. I mean, you get married and at some point a wife gets pregnant. I was somehow convinced it was just an automatic event. I figured the process couldn't have been as miraculous as the Immaculate Conception where Jesus was conceived in the womb of a virgin but the principle was pretty close. But while at school, my classmate Camille Johnson showed me in a Webster's dictionary how the whole sex thing went down. I absolutely could not believe it. I was floored, disappointed, indignant and offended all at the same time.

First, I thought I already knew how babies were conceived. In the fourth grade you don't want to be proven wrong about anything. Secondly, I was convinced that sex was somehow dirty. I knew about the sexual act, barely, but I was overwhelmingly persuaded that sex was sinful, wrong and forged and created by the dark lord Sauron. I couldn't imagine that Charles and Caroline Ingalls from "Little House on the Prairie" were having sex to give birth to Half Pint. Charles was too godly. There's no way my parents had sex one time let alone seven to give birth to me and my six siblings. My dad was a deacon in the Assembly of God church! No way. So, I came up with a new theory. There are now *two* ways that children were conceived instead of one. First, there was the natural way—God's way; and secondly there was the dirty way—the devil's way, as shown to me in the Webster's Dictionary by my demonized classmate.

How ridiculous, right? But here's the point: why in the world did I consider the definition of sexual intercourse as wrong? Where did I ever get the idea that babies came without sexual activity?

For some reason there was an inherent idea in my mind that sex was negative. It was already embedded in my thinking. Although at this point my dad and I had not had the sex talk, in their defense my parents certainly never taught me to believe anything like this. In other words, although I was untaught about the subject, I was not wrongly taught. My brain was just kind of made up for me. I had no real basis for my assumptions.

What if God was One of Us?

God is without argument the most misunderstood and mischaracterized Person in the world. People have this preconceived idea that God is mad, stingy and moody, if not non-existent altogether. Again, I grew up in church my whole life with good parents. However, I was fairly convinced deep down that God was irritated with me most of the time. Actually, I was pretty sure He was fed up with *most* of the people *most* of the time. Yes, He let out His entire wrath on His Son at the Cross but I was fairly certain He saved one last backhand especially for me. The problem was that I was never really sure when He was going to let me have it. Talk about breeding some insecurity!

Sure, there's some humor there, but it's reality for many Christians. Yet, God is not mad, unstable, or distant. He does not bring earthquakes to teach people a lesson. The idea that God is an angry God is a wrong viewpoint of Christian culture. God is good. God is light. God is love. Every good and perfect gift comes from the Father of Lights (James 1:17). God is consistent, faithful and trustworthy. He does not hate the world. God loves the world. God is not mad at you. God loves you. Yes, it's very true that God is powerful and hates sin. Yet, He primarily demonstrates His power in order to destroy sin over our lives to bring us into a place of freedom and relationship with Him. Goodness is His nature. Love is who He is. He richly gives us all things to enjoy, including sex.

God is Good: Sex is Good — That's Good News

Therefore, concerning God and sex, much of our wrong thinking and preconceived notions need to be undone. Most of us had our minds made up for us by the culture in which we were born. It does seem the norm that many untruths are inherited by the environment we live in. However the real danger is that any untruth we do not challenge is the lie we will be ruled by.

I was sexually aroused every day in the seventh grade! The girls in the eighth grade were quite different than the girls in the sixth grade. It was a miracle I didn't fall off the deep end. I thought I was a filthy pervert for all of the sexual thoughts and desires going on inside of me. Thank God during that year my dad gave me some help. He began to consistently tell me and my brothers, "Sex is good and God made it." He had seven kids so I figured he meant what he said. The second thing he did was give me an article written by Dr. James Dobson. It was directed to the young male adolescent who was going through the wild rush of change I was going through. Basically Dr. Dobson wrote that if you want to have sex then you are exactly where you should be. I thought, "What?!" He didn't stop there either. He went on to describe, respectfully, the intense pleasure of consummating the sexual act of intercourse. Wow! I wasn't some freak or sexual pervert. I was on the map now.

What a simple article; but how profound, and what an impact it made on me. Dr. Dobson illuminated me to the heart of our Creator and His original intent for sex. Also, the sense of validation I felt from God and my own father concerning my newfound sexual desire was huge because it spoke value to me at a most critical time in my life. As a young man in middle school I now knew that God made sex and it was good. These simple truths my dad directed me toward carried me a long way during my many *sex-less* years. They can for you too.

Original Intent

If you have some "stinkin' thinkin'" about God and sex, then the rest of this chapter will hopefully begin to bring some clarity. In order for us to understand the intent of something and to unlearn nuttiness, then we must go back to the owner's manual. For Christians that would be the Bible. Yes, young brother and sister, it would be good to read it and devour it. You don't need to wait until you're old and have nothing better to do. To add some incentive, please understand that the Scriptures have much to say about sex and the nature of the Author.

4

According to the *Webster's New Collegiate Dictionary*, "genesis" is defined as the *"origin of something."*[1] So, if you want find the origin of sex, go ahead and look at the book of Genesis *before sin and the fall of man.* The first two chapters say volumes concerning the nature of God and the blessing of sex. God makes His intent known rather quickly.

Here is what we see in a brief flurry of events: God spent five days making a perfect world and said, "It is good!" God spent day six making mankind and said, "It is very good!" God blesses Adam and puts him right in the middle of the awesome garden. Consider that God purposefully created everything first so that all would be ready for Adam once he opened his eyes for the first time. God gave Adam everything, including authority and power. He made Adam the boss of the earth under God's divine order. Adam said, "My life is good... *really good!*" Anyway, the point is, note God's wonderful nature and His heart to greatly bless his son. Next scene please:

This Girl Named Woman and this Guy Called Man

Now we're getting somewhere! Are you ready? God then creates the first woman. She is altogether perfect: in spirit, in soul, and yes, in body. The Bible says that God "brought her" to the man. Wow. What a moment that must have been: Adam was so overwhelmed that he prophesied her name!

Would you like to guess what happens next? **They have sex**. We see in verse twenty four that the Holy Spirit, the Author of the Holy Bible, states what transpires: *They became one flesh.* Adam and Eve had awesome sex in a literal perfect world. I would ask you to imagine what that must have been like but that would not be a good idea. But we do know that none of it was X-rated. It was all good! It was all God! It was all blessed! They got down to business in a lush garden.

Please do not feel in any way that the first sexual encounter in Scripture is being treated lightly or disrespectfully. That is not the intent whatsoever. Yes, becoming one flesh includes spiritual and emotional intimacy, including child conception. These are so emphatically important. Yet the primary point being made, at least in this book, is that sex is so spectacular, such a high priority of blessing, such an ever-flowing supply of power and pleasure, so much in the heart of God for his man and woman to enjoy together, that He includes it in the second chapter of the entire Bible. Listen closely: there are nearly 1,200 chapters in the Bible and God puts sex in chapter two!

This gift is for you. In God's original intent, sex is not dirty and there are no negative side effects. Holy sex... pleasurable sex... sex as He intended.

Many well-meaning American citizens would love to know how God votes. I'm going to give you that answer right now. Are you ready? God votes pro-sex.

You're in the Will of God for Wanting Sex

Young person, your time to "leave to cleave" is on the way. Just not yet! So, if this chapter got you a little fired up, go ahead and take a cold shower and order a hot pizza so we can move on to the next chapter. Let's pray together.

PRAYER:

Heavenly Father, I acknowledge that sex is good and that You made it to be a blessing in my life. I receive a new viewpoint of sex according to Your original intent. Wherever I have been obscured in my thinking or whatever lie I have believed concerning sex, I repent of it right now. I renounce any agreement I have made with these false ideas either directly or indirectly. I embrace Your report and receive the witness of Your Spirit in my thinking. Thank you for giving me Your perspective that sex is good. I pray this in Jesus name, Amen.

Chapter 2

No Cleavage "Till you Leave -age"
God's Great Expectations: Be Holy

*"Therefore shall a man **leave** his father and his mother, **and** shall **cleave** unto his wife: and they shall be one flesh."* (Genesis 2:24, KJV)

Yes, I think you know where we're going: no sex, right? Well, not exactly. As with any good gift that God gives His people, we can bet that the enemy of our souls will seek to pervert. Sex is one of the greatest gifts God ever gave man. We can therefore more easily understand why sex is so often misused. Sex has become a source of terrible abuse, perversion and destruction. Gifts are often abused when they are misused outside of their original intent. It's no wonder why sex is shrouded with negativity. It is for some of these reasons that God gives us instruction and boundaries to steward this blessing.

In the epic, testosterone filled movie *Gladiator*, there is a great scene where the Ethiopian warrior friend of Maximus is admonishing and encouraging the betrayed general of the Roman armies. He wanted to die and be reunited with his wife and son and freed from his anguish of soul. His words to Maximus concerning his family were this, *"You will meet them again, but not yet. Not yet!"*[1] So I would say to you that your time to enjoy the gift of sex is coming, but 'not yet... *not yet!*'

Sex, including all acts of sexual foreplay, has its appointment reserved exclusively at the marriage bed of covenant relationship. Translation? You can't have sex until you're married. Once again, nice and slow—sex is reserved for marriage. The answer isn't "*No*," it's "*Not yet*." God says in Genesis that only the young man that first leaves his parents' house will get to cleave to his new wife's body. In other words: No *leave-age*, no *cleavage* (or any other major skin exposure). No ring-*y*, no cling-*y*. Until you walk down the *aisle*, then you get no sex for a *while*. Keep your hands to *yourself* and put compromise and touching on the *shelf*. Unless the "I do's" are *said* then stay away from the *bed* (that includes a couch, back seats to a car, etc.). Keep your chonies on, your legs closed, and your hands to yourselves! *Comprende?*

This is where many feel that God is either unrealistic, living in the days of Moses or a stick in the mud. He is neither. First of all getting married as a virgin is not impossible. All kinds of people are doing it (you know what I mean). It's false to think it can't be done right. Again, God isn't unrealistic. He's given you everything that pertains to life and godliness (2 Peter 1:3).

Besides, God has His reasons why He commands his sons and daughters to flee sexual sin and His way is always best. He'll even tell you if you're diligent to ask Him about it. But sometimes you just have to obey and do what's right even though you don't fully understand. That can be tough especially when it seems like everyone else is getting away with having sex before marriage. Just know this: the Lord's promises to you are "Yes!" (2 Corinthians 1:20), including the one where you get married and have all the sex you want. His answer is yes, *just not yet*.

Standards and Expectations

"*Your priests violated My law and desecrated my holy things. They can't tell the difference between sacred and secular. They tell people there's no difference between right and wrong.*" (Ezekiel 22:26, MESSAGE)

When it comes to sexual activity before marriage there isn't all that much difference between the world and the Body of Christ. This is unfortunate but it is becoming more of an accurate fact. Sexual activity among unmarried Christian young adults is such that it has become the standard within our churches.

In *Every Young Man's Battle*, Stephen Arterburn and Fred Stoeker write that:

> *"Sex is everywhere—even in church settings. The custodial staff at my church has even found used condoms and torn condom wrappers in some classrooms in the mornings after youth group meetings. Can you believe that? While it sounds like I'm making this up, there's no reason to doubt that Christian youth are just as sexually active as their non-Christian peers. Surveys and research back it up."*[2]

In another instance my older brother shared with me a poll conducted in one of the weekend services in his "full gospel" church in 2009. Three thousand in attendance answered the question whether they believed sex outside of marriage was wrong or okay. Out of the three thousand Christians 63% marked on their polling card they believed sex outside of marriage was okay.

Let's not be so foolish to have a critical spirit toward anyone struggling with sexual sin; yet, it's important to emphasize the expectations of young adults in the Christian world. It is now the *expectation* for our young adults to be sexually active. It is no longer the *exception*. Even among some Christian parents is the expectation for their kids to be sexually active to some degree before they're married. As bad as the world is getting some Christian parents are just glad their kids didn't turn out to be an ax murderer! Sex before marriage is the least of their concerns. They'll even pass out the condoms! By all means use the condoms if you choose to be sexually active. However, although they may prevent venereal diseases, condoms will not negate the soul diseases that are guaranteed to follow. Once again, I'm not condemning the parents. I'm making a point concerning the current acceptance of sexual looseness.

Unfortunately, the destructive result of ignoring the sanctity of sex is that the majority of young adults will migrate toward the direction of the current standard and expectation of their peers. This would probably change if they could just see some role models step up to the plate, do what's right and lead by example. I know you understand that you're to be that example. So let's start right now and change this mindset of expectations.

Sexual Sin and How Far is Too Far

"Therefore, since Christ suffered in His body, arm yourselves also with the same attitude, because whoever suffers in the body is done with sin. As a result, they do not live the rest of their earthly lives for evil human desires, but rather for the will of God. For you have spent enough time in the past doing what pagans choose to do—living in... lust." (1 Peter 4:1-3, NIV)

In the New Testament, the Greek word *porneia* is defined as *sexual immorality* and encompasses, as a whole, all kinds of sexual sins. If you're not married *porneia* not only includes sexual intercourse but all sexual foreplay and fooling around, including heavy petting, masturbating someone else, oral sex, dry humping, and phone sex, just to name a few. We will discuss why sex sins are so destructive later but for now the standard for sexual purity is being raised again and made clear. Anything that intentionally stimulates sexual arousal in another person is sin.

So brother, if you think you have the goods, you can't sport your Speedos out on a date. You might cause your future wife to stumble...maybe stumble in laughter, but stumble nonetheless. I do say this as a joke since girls are not primarily visually driven as guys are. Typically girls are looking for an emotional connection and are drawn into sexual relationships by that *affection connection*. It's very different with guys who are intensely visually driven.

My sister, you already have the goods so you have to be extra careful. You have breasts, hips and thighs. There are enough curves in your body to make it difficult for a guy even if you're wearing an extra-large Glad bag on a date. You can't hide what God created you with but you are expected to be mindful and respectful so as not to intentionally make your brother in Christ unravel before your very eyes.

You can't press your chest together with a guy as you welcome him to church on Sunday morning with a hug. He's going to turn into the Incredible Hulk right there. Believe me when I say that no Avenger hero will be able to deliver him.

In the late 1990's my wife and I worked with the young adults at our church. The guys were great hearted young men that loved God and genuinely wanted to give God their best and honor Him. My wife and I often challenged them concerning sexual integrity and the dream to live for God's best in a future spouse. But the girls, some of them country girls, were just as corn fed as the boys, if you know what I mean. We had to teach them how to hug their brother and how to dress. So my sister, take it as a compliment as I encourage you to dress in a way that isn't unnecessarily distracting. This is one important way you can honor the Lord in your body.

God's Great Expectations: Be Holy

"Flee sexual immorality...do you not know that your body is the temple of the Holy Spirit who is in you, whom you have from God, and you are not your own? For you were bought at a price; therefore glorify God in your body and in your spirit, which are God's." (1 Corinthians 6:18-20)

The Word of God is our standard. We are to honor God in our bodies. How do we do that? Since our physical body is a temple of worship the Scriptures clearly tells us to abstain and flee sexual immorality. It does not matter if you feel like you're Elijah and *nobody* else seems to be living right (1 Kings 19:10). The Lord's expectation for you and me has not changed and will not. Culture, society, government policy or compromise among other Christians does not change the eternal Word of God and our responsibility to obey it. No finger pointing will be justified. You cannot blame your prodigal sibling, imperfect parents, your former youth pastor who ran off with another woman, or this broken world.

Please get this in your heart: *no cleavage till you leave-age.* God's original intent for sex must be stewarded and protected. God will hold you to account, but it will be worth it. As difficult as it may seem to wait sometimes, here's how I see it: God's standard for sex is as a crock pot is to tough tri-tip steak. God and His patient ways are the crock pot. His slow roasting ways can tenderize any meathead, such as yourself. Now, just go ahead and simmer down for a night so that tasty-lovin' and juicy joy will come in the morning. Until marriage, be holy.

PRAYER:

Father, help me to see clearly your standard for sexual integrity and to abide by it with all of my heart. I pray that You would fill me with zeal for Your temple, my physical body. I want to live by Your expectations for holiness. Forgive me for any level of compromise I have allowed or tolerated in my thoughts and behavior up until this point. I say 'Yes to sex... Just not yet!' I receive Your grace to forgive me and Your empowerment to obey. I say **no** *to any guilt, shame or condemnation and ask You to uproot any trace of it from my heart. I am excited and hopeful as I pursue intimacy with You and holiness in Jesus name, Amen.*

Chapter 3

Why Wait to Have Sex?
A Great Question!

I will never forget my dad making me and my little sister attend a Christian seminar for teens concerning premarital sex. The conservative denomination titled it, "*Why Wait?*" I was somewhat of a sarcastic teen back then and my response was, "Yeah. Good question. Why wait?!" It seemed to me that nobody else, who claimed to be Christian, was waiting to have sex and God wasn't striking them dead! Obviously my theology was off, too. Besides, God would forgive me. God could restore me. God wouldn't stop loving me.

So then, "*Why wait?*" became a very legitimate question in my mind. Why wait to have sexual foreplay until marriage? Why not engage in sexual intercourse? I mean shoot, the church choir will be singing "*Just as I Am*" while I walk down the sanctuary aisle to rededicate my life to the Lord after my season of sexual roller coasting fun. Why not eat, drink and fornicate and repent later? Why not Californicate in California while I'm California dreamin' on a winter's day with the California girls?

If you're asking yourself the same question minus the silliness I want you to know you're asking a good question that deserves to be answered. God is more than willing to speak to this and He is not exasperated about any possible frustrations you may have. He will give you wisdom as you seek Him with a sincere heart without making you feel belittled or selfish for asking (James 1:5). He invites us to reason with Him (Isaiah 1:18). If God patiently put up with Jonah's bitterness, Elijah's misguided conclusions, Gideon's ding dong fleeces and the prodigal's brother's hardness—surely God will lovingly and patiently help us.

Seriously, Why Wait?

I want to give you some good solid reasons to help you in your decision making about waiting to have sex from this moment forward until you're married. Some may not sound too sexy (no pun intended) but coupled with a heart that wants to please God and do what's right, they might serve as an authentic encouragement for you. I know we agree when we say we can use as much help as we can get. Let's look at a few: Don't have sex before marriage because...

It's right: The Bible says that sex is reserved for marriage. Simply put, it is the right thing to do to wait to have sex until you're married. It may not seem fair or sufficient to satisfy your questions or bitterness but it is, nevertheless, significant. To do what is right when you cannot see the big picture, or when it seems like nobody else is doing it right, or when no one else is watching or giving you props, goes a long way with God.

Samuel is one of the most powerful pictures of this principle in all of the Scriptures. He inspired me a great deal during all my many *sex-less* years. A little backdrop: Samuel ministered before the Lord as a priest from his early childhood but he was surrounded by intense sexual compromise. Eli was priest while the tabernacle was in Shiloh and his whore-mongering sons, Hophni and Phinehas, served as priests with their father. The two brothers, among other things, would fornicate with the women who would assemble to serve in the basic tasks at the tabernacle. Not good! That's like having sex in the church sanctuary while the rest of the congregation is worshipping and receiving Holy Communion. Scary stuff for sure. However, here this whole time Samuel chose not to be influenced by them. He held fast to his integrity. The Bible says:

> "...the child Samuel grew in stature and in favor both with the Lord and with men...and ministered to the Lord." (1 Samuel 2:26, 3:1)

14

He was faithful when others around him were not. Did you catch that? Another noteworthy characteristic was that this young hero did what was right *before* he ever knew or experienced the Lord in a personal and direct way (Samuel 3:7). In other words Samuel didn't obey the Lord because he had the presence of God on him so powerfully or had angelic manifestations or the promise of seven virgins if he stayed away from fornication. He did what was right without having the goose bump spiritual experiences. That was not his motivation for obedience. Basically, Samuel knew he had been dedicated to the Lord from birth and chose to honor that dedication through right conduct. He was not floating in the air or glowing in the dark because of the glory of God in His life.

Perhaps some of you can identify with what Samuel went through. Although I was raised in church, I rarely sensed God's personal touch. Of course it's not that God was holding back. Maybe my hardened heart, critical attitude and pride had something to do with it. I'm not so sure. But as I grew into my late teens I made the decision to really give God my best and pursue His will for my life with everything I had. However, I still found myself having to obey Him concerning "no sex" simply because the Book said so, my conscience agreed and because it was the right thing to do. At times this greatly frustrated me because I wanted more answers, more glitter and powerful prophecies. I struggled with resentment as I would observe compromise from others in the Christian circles. But what can help hold us steady during these seasons of testing is the integrity of doing what's right even when nobody is cheering for you. I assure you, when you feel that way, God is cheering for you. He is saying over you like He did in 1 Samuel 2:35:

> *"I will raise up for Myself a faithful priest, who shall do what is according to what is in My heart and in My mind. I will build him a sure house, and he shall walk before My anointed forever."*

Be assured that heaven is taking notice as you endeavor to do what is right.

It's better to obey: Read 1 Samuel 15:22 to understand what the prophet was saying when he spoke these words to King Saul, *"Behold, to obey is better than sacrifice."*

Again, it was my experience as a teen that the church spent so much of their efforts tending to the people who were sinning that there wasn't much love for the people trying to live right. In other words, the focus of ministry was more on recovering from the sacrifice that comes with sin, to the point that there wasn't much said about the blessings of obedience. The message of grace seemed to only lean toward forgiveness but not to the other side: the empowerment to obey and overcome.

There should be a healthy balance. When we struggle with sin, there is mercy. If we accept the challenge to pursue sexual purity, there should be exciting ministry and authentic vision to inspire you. You should be hearing that it's better to obey and overcome than it is to sin and have to be restored. Why? Because God said that life is better when you obey. You will be happier. There will be less stress. The drama that follows multiple boy or girlfriends and sexual activity is off the charts. Skip the drama. Your motto should be "Yo-mama to the drama." This might be a good T-Shirt idea. No pictures though.

Try to keep it simple and obey the Bible. Do it God's way. Yes, there will be some persecution and pressure for your obedience but it is absolutely nothing to be compared with His glory to be revealed in you (2 Corinthians 4:17) in this life and the next. I know you want a better life. Your key is to obey.

Your life is His testimony in the earth: You represent Jesus Christ. He is at the right hand of the Father wanting to show Himself strong through you in your circle of influence. It is your responsibility, with God's help, to represent Him in an honorable way. Sin brings reproach to God and misrepresents Him before people. Most non-Christians don't like God because of compromising Christians. People are watching you. You may be the closest a person may ever get to the Lord. Your not having sex right now may be the last thread of hope for someone who is almost convinced that all Christians are hypocrites.

"He who heeds instruction and correction is [not only himself] in the way of life [but also] is a way of life for others. And he who neglects or refuses reproof [not only himself] goes astray [but also] causes to err and is a path toward ruin for others." (Proverbs 10:17, AMP).

Continued sexual sin brings reproach to our testimony. If you're fooling around sexually and you're out sharing your faith in Christ openly, you will damage the conscience of unbelievers and believers alike. There is nothing you can do about your past sexual activity. God specializes in the redeeming business. However, now is your hour to shine as His light. Living with sexual integrity is a huge way we can live as a testimony for Jesus Christ. Be wise and choose the fear of the Lord. The world needs Jesus Christ but we, the Church, are His delivery system in the earth. Let your light shine and be a faithful testimony by abstaining from all forms of sexual activity.

1 Corinthians 9:27 says, *"But [like a boxer] I buffet my body [handle it roughly, discipline it by hardships] and subdue it, for fear that after proclaiming to others the Gospel and things pertaining to it, I myself should become unfit [not stand the test, be unapproved and rejected as a counterfeit]"* (AMP).

You are not a counterfeit Christian so live right. Do it for Jesus. You are His testimony.

Jesus shed His blood: Our Lord became the Lamb of God. He was brutally beaten and crucified on a sinner's cross. He bore the sin of mankind. He became a curse. Jesus' body was broken and His blood was shed in our behalf. Therefore, what response should we have?

1 Corinthians 6:19-20 says it well, *"Do you not know that your body is the temple of the Holy Spirit who is in you, whom you have from God, and you are not your own? 20 For you were bought at a price; therefore glorify God in your body and in your spirit, which are God's."*

Verse 17 of the same chapter clearly states that we should flee all forms of sexual sin. Choose to not give yourself the right to take the temple of God, your body, which was purchased at the expense of the blood of Jesus, and abuse it through sexual sin. Because of the price paid to make our body His temple, I believe you would agree that God deserves our obedience.

Sexual lust cannot deliver on its promises: Lust talks. Lust is an embellishing liar. Lust will try to sell you ocean front property in Arizona and throw the Golden Gate in for free to get you to buy into its seduction. However lust cannot deliver. Sexual lust will not satisfy.

> This is what sexual **lust promises** to its potential customer: *Stolen water is sweet, and bread eaten in secret is pleasant.*

> This is what **lust delivers**: *But he does not know that the dead are there, that her guests are in the depths of hell.* (Proverbs 9:17-18)

Sexual lust **might not** send you to hell but it will **certainly** unleash hell into your soul and life while you're here on earth. Bet on it. Yielding to lust will not make you a stud, a desirable woman, well rounded (except for becoming pregnant) or build your self-esteem. Sin will produce shame and death. Any decision or act toward sexual lust is a seed sown to build up your sin nature. Feeding that particular lust appetite will produce exponential dominance of your flesh. That flesh or lower nature is not the real you, but will take on a greater influence in your life until you become more mindful of the things of the flesh rather than the Spirit (Romans 8:5). The lower nature is filled with the works of the flesh (Galatians 5:19-21). One translation describes the flesh as having animal like impulses. You are not an animal so don't let the flesh or the devil make you feel or act like one.

Sexual lust is a liar and a thief. It will attempt to seduce you into compromise, and then mock you after you've been duped. Your body is God's dwelling place. You have the power of the Holy Spirit in you to put to death the deeds of the flesh (Romans 8:13). You have authority over all the power of the enemy (Luke 10:19), including lust.

You were recreated in Christ Jesus to win. Sexual lust is far beneath your elevated place in God through Christ (Ephesians 1). Sexual lust has nothing that you need. You will win by not playing the game. Don't even go there. Again, sex, sex, and more sex are in your future: just not on the world, the flesh or the devil's terms. Sexual lust cannot deliver.

The pleasure of sin is temporary: Let's be clear: sexual sin is pleasurable. You don't need the devil or the flesh to tell you that! You don't need to eat of the Tree of the Knowledge of Good and Evil to find this out. Why? Because the Tree of Life already tells us! Hebrews 11:25 says that Moses chose to obey God rather than *"enjoy the passing pleasures of sin."* The point is that sexual sin is pleasurable and enjoyable. This is clear Scripture. So when the devil whispers in your ear and says, "Oh, you know you want it!" Say back to him, "Oh yes! You have no idea!" Yet, there is a higher truth and a more persuasive influence here: the pleasure of sexual sin is very temporary. It lasts as long as the sexual experience and that's about it. However, the implications of sexual sin last a whole lot longer. The pleasure of sexual sin is fleeting but God's favor is for life. There's no comparison.

You may not recover from sexual sin: What?! It's true, unfortunately. Some people never get out of the iniquity cycle of sexual sin. If you're thinking that you can have sex now and repent later, then think again. What makes you so sure that you will resist *later* the same temptation you choose not to resist *today*? Sowing to the sexual appetite only increases the appetite. It will be more difficult later to resist than today. People who consistently sow to the flesh while ignoring the loving conviction of the Holy Spirit can eventually become so overrun by the flesh that they won't want to fight the battle and will therefore forfeit the war.

> *"Don't you realize that you become the slave of whatever you choose to obey? You can be a slave to sin, which leads to death, or you can choose to obey God, which leads to righteous living."* (Romans 6:16, NLT)

Paul is talking to Christians here. These self-inflicted chains binding the believer can absolutely be broken to pieces. The issue is with us, however, not with God. This isn't a matter of whether or not God will have mercy and forgive us. The issue is: Will we receive His mercy and repent of the sin pattern? We hold the keys of authority and exercise the power to choose. God is always faithful and just to forgive us and cleanse us of all unrighteousness (1 John 1:9). However mercy is contingent on our confession of the sin and our forsaking it.

> "*He who covers his sins will not prosper but whoever* **confesses and forsakes** *them will have mercy.*" (Proverbs 28:13)

We have the final say. We cast the deciding vote. We have been given the right to choose life or death. The implications of sexual sin run deeper than any other sin (1 Corinthians 6:18). Don't stand toe to toe with sexual immorality. Flee and abstain. You might not choose to repent later.

You would prefer your little sister do the same: How do you want young men to treat your little sister? If you have a little sister you know where I'm headed. This is what I faced in my late teen years during my several month crossroads. I challenged myself and asked, "What if the way I was to treat young women was the same exact way other guys would treat my little sister?"

During that season in my life I was very close to going down the path of the dark side of sexual whoredom. I was being seduced by the power of the ring. I could see Sauron of *Lord of the Rings* and lord Sidias of *Star Wars* beckoning me by name and promising me shared rulership of both the entire Galaxy and Middle Earth. A little dramatic I know but I was genuinely in the fight of my life and in the valley of decision. Actually, I was very close to going over the deep end and tossing away my virginity and becoming a whoremonger, just like my older brothers. I'll give you their full names a little later so you can Google them.

In all seriousness I had to focus and make a decision during this absolutely critical moment in my life. Destiny was, for sure, hanging in the balance and I knew it. It was at this time I was challenged with this thought concerning my little sister, Rebecca. Obviously I wanted my sister to be treated honorably and to be honorable herself. Therefore, partly inspired by my sister, I chose not to date until the right one came along and not treat females in a dishonorable way. Sure, it was just a small act of integrity but I had no idea the impact those decisions would have on me or my sister. I also was clueless as to how closely she was watching me and my choices. She was going through her own valley of decision at the same time.

When I made an about-face to give God everything, she followed right after. 1Timothy 5:2 says that men are to "*treat younger women with all purity as you would your own sisters*" (NLT).

You would prefer your future spouse do the same:

> "*Therefore, whatever you want men to do to you, do also to them, for this is the Law and the Prophets.*" (Matthew 7:12)

Whoever and wherever your future spouse is, I imagine how you would like for them to behave sexually. That's a good desire. God made you that way. Don't think yourself to be selfish or a religious freak for wanting your spouse to be a virgin when you get married. To have standing next to you at the altar of marriage someone sexually pure is a precious gift. However, my question to you is this: how are *you* behaving? Your conduct with those of the opposite sex should reflect what you would like to see in your future spouse.

First of all, seek to honor the Lord in your body because you love Him and desire to honor Him. This commitment is regardless of the decisions of your future spouse. Even if they are choosing to live in a manner inconsistent with the Scriptures it still does not negate your responsibility before God. Your honor and joy come from Him, not the conduct of your future mate.

With that said, God's heart and original intent is for a man and a woman to be completely sexually pure on their wedding day. The value of virginity is priceless so start today. Sexual activity with someone who is not your spouse is stealing. You are touching someone else's future husband or wife. Therefore act in a manner you would have your marriage partner to act. It's part of the Law and the Prophets. If you *want* that in your future mate then *be* that for your future mate.

You can make up for lost time after you're married: You may not be having sex for the next few years but one of the opportunities you have is to make up for lost time by having a plethora of sex *after* you're married. When my wife and I were engaged and I would deny my flesh its appetite to take a bite out of my wife-to-be before marriage, I would talk back to my flesh. I let myself know how much I wanted sex however not on its terms. I also would talk to the devil since it seemed he was talking to me all the time. I invited him to my honeymoon but he never showed up. He has a hard time being present where the glory of God dwells.

There were a few articles of clothing I wanted my future wife to wear after we were married just for the mere reason of taking them off. There was only one time in our entire eighteen month engagement that when I picked her up for a date I told her she couldn't wear what we she was wearing. The clothes were presenting a believable case to me how they were meant for the floor and not for her body. I took a mental note and said to that sexy outfit: "I will see you again after our honeymoon and will repay you for your trash talking! I'm going to handle you like a scratch and sniff and rip you off of her body with my bare teeth!" Obviously, I fully intended to make up for lost time. Sixteen years later I want you to know that I've kept my word.

You will be so glad you did: Time flies. You'll be married and having all kinds of sex in no time. You will be so deeply thankful you waited to have sex until marriage. If you have been sexually active until this point you will be so blessed to look back and know that you made the right adjustments. Every right decision you make from this point on can help restore honor, integrity, wholeness and a healthy sense of innocence. A lot of your personal healing will be found in your present obedience. 1 Peter 1:22 says that our souls are purified through obedience. Our King is a redeemer and can fill you with joy and a sense of accomplishment and victory instead of regret and disappointment. You will be glad you did.

You're not like everybody else: Isn't it interesting that we all want to be our own person, yet try to justify ourselves to have premarital sex because everyone else is? So why wait to have sex? Simple: You're *not* like everybody else! You have been fearfully and wonderfully made. Before you were ever born God already knew you and set you apart for His specific purposes and pleasure (Jeremiah 1:5). You do not touch others sexually and do not allow yourself to be touched because you are separate and holy to the Lord. The masses in the churches are active sexually. Be who God made *you* to be and live how He called *you* to live.

Do *not* judge and do *not* point the finger but ***do not*** do what they do. Maybe they need you to *not* be like them so you eventually will be able to *help* them. Having sex because others are is no reason to have sex.

Shadrach, Meshach and Abednigo didn't bow because they were not like everybody else. Moses didn't enjoy the passing pleasures of sin because he was not like everybody else. Daniel wouldn't stop praying because he was not like everybody else. David took off the giant's head because he was not like everybody else. Joshua made the sun stand still because he was not like everybody else. Elijah outran the horse, Elisha split open the Jordan, Rahab defied the king of Jericho, Enoch was taken to heaven, Abraham killed five kings, Isaac had a hot wife, Jacob wrestled with God, Joseph didn't touch Potiphar's wife, Samuel's words didn't fall to the ground, Solomon was unsurpassed in wisdom, Josiah destroyed the high places, Jeremiah continued to prophesy, Esther went before the king without being summoned, Ezra built the temple, Nehemiah built the wall, Jesus was born of a virgin, John danced for joy in his mother's womb, the disciples left all to follow the Man of Galilee, Peter walked on the water, Paul praised his way out of the prison, John loved his way out of boiling oil… why?! It was *because they were not like everybody else!*

Neither are you. You're someone great in the eyes of God and are mighty in this earth. You're no cookie cutter girl or dull boy. Your contribution in the earth to your generation cannot be duplicated. This is one of the reasons why you will wait until your wedding night to wear yourself out with sex. You're not like everybody else! For all of these reasons, you can wait. The devil is a liar. Yes, you can.

PRAYER:

Dear Lord, from this moment forward, I truly desire to wait to have any sexual activity until marriage. I choose to live at the highest possible level of integrity for Your honor and also for my benefit. May all of the reasons and Your incentives to do so burn brightly in me and provide me with strengthening motivation. May my relationship with You be so rich and satisfying that it more than compensates for the wait. Enlarge my vision. Keep me in the fear of the Lord. I thank You and praise You for it now in Jesus name, Amen.

Chapter 4

What Happens in Vegas Doesn't Stay in Vegas
Sexual Sin Runs Deep

"Shun...all sexual looseness [flee from impurity in thought, word, or deed]. Any other sin which a man commits is one outside the body, but he who commits sexual immorality sins against his own body." (1 Corinthians 6:18, AMP)

Obviously we're on to more serious things now. It's all fun and games until we start talking about consequences. Yes, they do exist. No, consequences have nothing to do with God being mad at you or making you pay for not doing things His way. As you know they are the direct result of our own actions. We don't need to bother getting offended with God for the consequences of our own bad decisions. This desperately needs to be clearly voiced in our present culture of entitlement.

If you could use a little more motivation to live with sexual integrity then this chapter might sober you up toward obedience. God does not initiate fear tactics to move us toward Him. However, in a moment after seeing the hellish effects of sin and the deceitfulness of our own flesh, you might just be scared into doing what's right. Disobedience has deadly repercussions and opens us up to all kinds of unwanted garbage. Although it's not fun, this is a necessary pit stop on this guide toward integrity.

There was a commercial some time back advertising the Las Vegas entertainment industry. The idea was to attract more tourists to the city. It aired people having a wild time and ended with the line, "*What happens in Vegas... stays in Vegas.*" But be sure about this; what happens in Vegas *does not stay* in Vegas! It never has. It's also the same with sexual sin. Unfortunately, it doesn't stay in Vegas. It is not an isolated event.

Sexual sin stays in you and with you. Thoughts, sounds, acts, partners and fantasy tend to become ingrained in the minds of those involved. Soul ties will always knot up its participants. Sexual sins are simply worse than others. Their implications run deeper. It's not that God is cursing or punishing people who sin. Rather it is partly a consequence to the misuse of the blessing of sex. The greater the blessing we are given then greater is the responsibility. The misuse of greater responsibilities leads to more devastating and longer lasting repercussions. The spiritual law of sowing and reaping works on the positive and on the negative side, either to bless or produce consequences.

It appears that once awoken, the sexual appetite takes extreme dedication and discipline to silence and keep crucified. Consider below the Physical Intimacy Scale from the book *Relationships,* by Dr.'s Les and Leslie Parrot:

1. Embracing and hand holding
2. Cuddling and gentle caressing
3. Polite kissing on the lips
4. Passionate total mouth kissing
5. Intense and prolonged total mouth kissing
6. Fondling breasts and genitals outside the clothes
7. Fondling breasts and genitals under the clothes
8. Oral or genital stimulation to orgasm outside the clothes
9. Oral or genital stimulation to orgasm under the clothes
10. Sexual intercourse

Obviously most of this is sinful sex if you're not married. Furthermore, this husband-and-wife team goes on to note that "*anytime you move past stage five it becomes exponentially more difficult to maintain control.*"[1] Again, it doesn't take much arousal to drag us into the mayhem of sexual sin. Without diligence, once tripped up, it doesn't take too long to become totally entangled by this web. Sexual iniquity is a horrible path filled with all kinds of pain. Unfortunately, to add to the devastation, immorality leads to many other sins as well.

The Knock-Out Punch of Sexual Sin

In suspense or mystery movies we see the wicked villain grab their victim and quickly place over their face a handkerchief doused with the colorless and heavy toxic liquid called chloroform. Immediately the victim becomes unconscious and is taken advantage of or held captive. Sexual sin is like that chloroform to the believer. It's a knockout punch unlike any other. It messes people up and brings all kinds of disillusionment.

More so than other sins, when you violate the boundaries concerning sex, you enter into a vague world that will take you out of the driver's seat of your life. You are not yourself at this point. Many are in this prison and it leads down a path to steep moral, emotional and spiritual decline. It is a deceiving downward spiral of bondage and it doesn't take much to draw you in. When you finally come out the other side, you'll be so backwards you'll put your right shoe on your left foot, hairspray under your arm pits, brush your teeth with hemorrhoid cream and wonder what's wrong with everybody else.

The Merriam-Webster's New Collegiate Dictionary describes the effects of chloroform as to "*produce anesthesia, insensibility or death.*"[2] After the chloroform of immorality, people will find themselves doing things they never would have imagined prior to the sin. They have now become *insensible*.

Many good people, before committing adultery, would have never imagined putting themselves, their children or family through such hell. Yet, after adultery, they will even justify their behavior and leave the children to deal with the terrible ordeal of an affair and divorce. They justify themselves as the victim, instead of taking the most basic responsibility for their actions. The idea of such behavior would have been unthinkable years before. How is it possible to go from one extreme to the other? They got knocked out with sexual sin. Furthermore, the Bible also calls this *the deceitfulness of sin*. We are all susceptible to it.

You see, you cannot flirt with sexual sin and win. You cannot be sexually active as a Christian and somehow think you're holding your own. That is impossible. Remember this truth, that *sin takes you farther than you wanted to go, keeps you longer than you wanted to stay and costs you more than you're willing to pay.*

The Scriptures do not lay out in full detail why sexual sin has such a terribly unique devastation on a person. We just know that it does. Dr. Jack Hayford, author of *Fatal Attractions: Why Sex Sins are Worse than Others*, wrote:

> *"The Word of God declares, 'None of us lives to himself, and no one dies to himself' (Romans 14:7), putting forever to rest society's pathetic notion that by engaging in sex sin, "I'm not hurting anyone but myself." But sexual sin becomes as toxic, as invasive, as hereditary, as transferable and as ruinous as cancer. The Bible provides both warnings and case history to evidence the damaging consequences of sexual indulgence, disobedience to God's laws and irresponsible behavior upon others, not just upon oneself."*[3]

When the Apostle Paul details the works of the flesh in Galatians chapter 5, he spells out over a dozen manifestations, or acts, of the sin nature. The first one is, unsurprisingly, sexual immorality. Romans chapter 1 reveals people saturated with sins such as being heartless, inventors of new forms of evil, secret backbiters, full of cruel ways, strife, envy, jealousy and eventually murder. These individuals matured into these depths of twisted behavior but interestingly had their beginning with sexual immorality. These people that once had knowledge of God were handed over to:

*"...the lusts of their own hearts to **sexual impurity**, to the dishonoring of their bodies...**until** they were filled (permeated and saturated) with every kind of unrighteousness, iniquity."* (Romans 1:24, 29, AMP)

It's clear: **sexual impurity has the potential to lead to every kind of unrighteousness**. It's not that sexual sin is unforgivable. However, it's often the doorway that opens the floodgates to many other sins as well. It starts here and once again can ultimately lead to the extreme of murder. Unfortunately, we have all heard of stories where this line of progressive conduct played out.

Stages of Conscience Violations

With each successive decision to persist in sexual sin, the mind of the believer increases in darkness. Sin is an act of darkness and, without repentance, will keep a believer in darkness. With that said, it seems like there is a Biblical pattern of a moral decline that leads to strongholds, hard heartedness and conscience conflicts in the lives of good, young believers. I don't particularly enjoy this part of the book but it's necessary, so let's consider a few progressive stages of the conscience.

Pure or clear conscience: The person who has steered clear of sexual activity has a fairly clear conscience concerning sexual sin. Having a clear conscience and being naïve is not the same thing.

Romans 16:19 says, *"I would have you well versed and wise as to what is good and innocent and guileless as to what is evil."* (AMP)

Do not believe the lie that if you have lived a holy or sexually pure life that you have no real testimony or can't help anybody. That is obviously not true. Part of your persecution will be that those, even in the church, might inadvertently make you feel that you can't help anybody if you've never lived sinfully. It's incorrect, but at times is unfortunately directly or indirectly implied by Christians. If this thinking were true, then Daniel, Samuel and Esther would have been unqualified to be used by God to help their imperfect generation. Joseph, with his clean record, would have been off God's team. Even Jesus would have been ineffective! This line of thinking is ridiculous. I know people who have blown their virginity over that lie. They went ahead and had sex to try to earn their testimony.

God will use a pure and holy life to minister to many. Obedience qualifies a believer to testify. Your innocence is a mighty presence against the enemies of God and increases your witness. It is a blessed life to be clear in conscience: more filling, less drama.

Convicted or violated conscience: If a person chooses to involve themselves in an initial sexual act like petting then the conscience will be violated. This is when you know you have crossed a line and a part of you feels violated. Although this experience could have been consensual and pleasurable, typically following the experience a person feels a host of negative emotions like guilt, regret and shame. They cannot escape this conviction: "*This was wrong.*" What happens at this point is important. Will the believer repent or instead continue and go deeper into sin?

You might hear that subtle voice say, "*See, you sinned but God forgave you. You can still feel His love, can't you? You don't even have to confess your sin to anyone. You've repented to God and that's enough. You can keep dating this person. It won't happen again.*" The enemy and your own sin nature will work hard to keep you from confessing that sin to another believer and thereby bringing that sin out into the light (1 John 1). Through genuine and heartfelt confession of sin, a believer will move toward freedom and cleansing. Although no one is perfect we are grateful that God is faithful.

However, a lack of coming clean will cause a stronghold to be established. If there's no real repentance then this person will probably move farther down the intimacy scale. Hopefully obedience is the choice. If not, they have awoken their sexual appetite and will more than likely be led right back to the same sin and worse.

Condemned, weak or defiled conscience: As the strength of the Spirit's conviction lessens, this person slides farther into the bondage of sin and the adversary takes more ground in the heart of the believer. Repetitive sin authorizes the enemy to hold captive a part of our mind through deception.

> *"Leave no [such] room or foothold for the devil [give no opportunity to him]."* (Ephesians 4:27, AMP)

On the flip side we clearly see in this passage that through ignorance or willful sin we can give the enemy room in our lives. Where the Word of God was meant to occupy there is now wrong thinking. The word *defile* in the Greek literally means *soiled*. So now you have a Christian whose got stinkin' thinkin' because they have a room in their brain that's filled with "dookie" through willful sin. This is what happens when we know to do good but do not do it (James 4:17).

Thankfully we have the God factor. He is always willing to redirect us through His loving conviction. He can illuminate us to our wavering condition and bring light, truth and mercy. However, once again we have a decision to make. Unfortunately, the tears that were shed after the initial sin encounter could quickly fade into a mild, "I know this isn't right but *'what do you expect?'*" More than likely, this person will soon begin to engage in sexual intercourse.

Seared conscience: This believer is firmly defeated in this area of their life and the wall of their soul is broken down. They continue dating knowing their self-control is at an all-time low. Some believers slide deeper into a horrible web of iniquity called *lasciviousness*. This word generally means an "absence of restraint" and is a work of the flesh according to Galatians 5:19. A good young believer can spiral into this depth of depravity because of repeatedly ignoring promptings of the Holy Spirit. Instead, they consistently acted on the impulses of their flesh and a terrible sin pattern emerged.

I knew a girl my senior year in high school who loved God and was in a good church. Her boyfriend was a believer, too. After falling in love and after six months of dating they gave their virginity to each other. They broke up shortly after, due to the drama that, unsurprisingly, followed. This girl never recovered and began the decline into lasciviousness. Six months after her break up, she had sex with another guy on their very first date. Notice: this attractive girl lived as a believing virgin for seventeen years and fell to the pressure of sexual temptation. Yet, after that experience, she was nearly without restraint only after several months.

Keep in mind that by this time people are not so much acting intentionally. They're knocked out. Although they are responsible for their actions they are not firing on all cylinders. Also remember, we're not talking only about the world but also those in the Body of Christ. Listen to Paul's words in Ephesians 4:19:

> "In their spiritual apathy they have become callous and past feeling and reckless and **have abandoned themselves** [a prey] to unbridled sensuality, eager and greedy to indulge in **every form of impurity [that their depraved desires may suggest and demand]**." (AMP)

Absolutely nothing or no one can fill an empty heart except Jesus Christ. Feeling unwanted and depressed leads many to sexual promiscuity. Carnal desires should not rule us, but when we fall deeper into sexual sin we are giving away a part of our true selves until there isn't much left, including the fruit of the Spirit called self-control. If our lives have been sown repeatedly toward the flesh then the weakness of our sin nature will dominate the willingness of our spirit. At this point, a person can become almost totally self-and-sense-ruled.

Debased or reprobate: This is when the floodgates of filthy sin and demonic defilement are totally open and flowing. The second half of Romans chapter two describes the depravity. This is where nearly every form of vile sexual sin and perversion is unleashed but now it is accompanied by a twisted justification for the behavior. Now this believer is willingly sold to their flesh. At this point they don't even want to retain God in their knowledge.

"Now the Spirit expressly says that in latter times some will depart from the faith, giving heed to deceiving spirits and doctrines of demons, speaking lies in hypocrisy, having their own conscience seared with a hot iron." (1 Timothy 4:1-2)

Sin Doesn't Stay in Vegas

Ay caramba! This stuff is no joke and is bad news anyway you look at it. To make matters worse sin also attracts harassing demonic activity. Through constant disobedience a believer can move themselves out from under a measure of God's protection. Remember: God does not pull back from us. The power to choose to draw near or away from God is ours. He doesn't force our obedience and He's not beating us up for sin. The pain a believer is experiencing is the penalty that sin itself is producing. God isn't a schizophrenic. He's not a passive-aggressive Father punishing you indirectly for your sin. God loves you so much and wants to help you no matter what stage of health your conscience is in.

Consider this: through King Saul's persistent disobedience and fear of man, he invited a tormenting spirit to practically drive him insane (1 Samuel 16:14). Samuel referred to Saul's constant rebellion as witchcraft in chapter fifteen. Did you hear that? Rebellion is like divination. Cain's half-hearted devotion to God and his ensuing anger became sin for him (Genesis 4). His anger then attracted a spirit of murder. He could have ruled over it but he was overcome instead.

On a side note, here's a clue: if you struggle with panic attacks, do not be watching horror movies. Also, even if you *do not* suffer from panic attacks, do not be watching horror movies! You might attract to yourself a demonic spirit of fear by your own invitation. Furthermore, consistent sexual sin will attract sexually unclean demonic harassment. People deal with foul dreams, harassing sexual torments, and a driving and overbearing pressure to sin. The Bible says that when we do not fully obey the Lord but allow persistent sin to remain, then that sin will later be like *"irritants in your eyes and thorns in your sides, and they shall harass you"* (Number 33:55-56).

Sexual immorality doesn't stay in Vegas. This sin business is dirty. The world, the flesh and the devil are ripping people to shreds. I can't encourage you enough to avoid this entire mess. Song of Solomon 2:7 says, *"Don't excite love, don't stir it up, until the time is ripe"* (MESSAGE). There is a proper time, which is marriage, for sexual desire to reach its fulfillment.

God wants to help you. He is bigger than it all. It's never over or too late. Let's get cleaned up, healed up, get away and stay away from all this. Sound good?

If you struggle with fear, any kind of torment or challenge with sleeping peacefully, there is sleep aid recording I encourage you to purchase entitled *Knightime Prayers for Teens and Young Adults*. It is a forty-minute prayer accompanied by anointed background music that is designed to strengthen you while you're awake and bring the peace of God as you go to sleep. The prayer covers your sleep, the spiritual and physical environment of your home, protection, your destiny and relationships. You can get it at most Christian bookstores, download it from iTunes or order it from www.reachingforwardmedia.com. There have been many legitimate testimonies of our King bringing His peace to struggling young people through this recording. That's the objective. Our Lord is a mighty redeemer. If you're coming to Him for help He's not going to leave you suffering saying, "Well, you made your bed now sleep in it!" That's not our God. Let's run to Him right now as we pray together.

PRAYER:

Heavenly Father I am in need of Your help and I am boldly asking for it. I want to draw close to You and I sincerely desire to obey You. Deliver me out of this pit. I do not want to live for myself. Please make my conscience tender once again. Create in me a clean heart and renew a steadfast spirit within me. Forgive me where I have sinned against You and others. I receive the power of the Holy Spirit right now to free me, work in me and use me to help others. Also, I receive Your love to settle my mind and give me peace. I choose the fear of the Lord that strengthens me to depart from evil. Thank You for it all in Jesus name, amen.

Chapter 5

High Places and Strongholds
Everybody Ain't Doing it

*"You shall **utterly destroy all the places** where the nations which you shall dispossess served their gods, on the **high mountains** and on the hills and under every green tree. And you shall **destroy** their altars, **break** their sacred pillars, and **burn** their wooden images with fire; you shall **cut down** the carved images of their gods and **destroy** their names from **that place**. You shall not worship the LORD your God with such things."* (Deuteronomy 12:2-4)

Old Testament High Places

A re you ready for a bit of a study? What we're about to look at is important. Hopefully this chapter will stoke the fire of the warrior in you. Let's get started.

During the time of the Judges, Israel, God's chosen people, adopted the pagan custom of offering sacrifices at high places or elevated hilltops. The pagans or Gentiles (non-Israelite) believed the closer they were to heaven, the greater the chance their prayer and sacrifices would reach their gods. Since many of these high places were old Baal (demon deity) sites, this practice was expressly forbidden to the Israelites (Leviticus 17:3, 4).

God did, however, appear to give one exception and that was the great high place at Gibeon where the Tabernacle of Moses resided. This is where men like Samuel and Solomon worshipped with God's approval, especially since the first temple had not yet been built (1 Samuel 9:12-14, 1 Kings 3:2, Deuteronomy 12:13-14). After these exceptions in the early years of Israel's history, the high places were off limits to God's people. This was especially true after the temple was built and all Israel could come and worship the Lord in Jerusalem.

Nevertheless, in King Solomon's later years, after the temple was finished, he built high places of false worship for his pagan wives. Remember, Solomon went a little nutty after the chloroform of too much sex with too many foreign women. According to 1 Kings, chapter 11, we see that from these high places Solomon and his pagan wives worshipped several gods. Interestingly enough, one of them was Ashtoreth, the Canaanite goddess of fertility, whose worship primarily involved illicit sex.

High Places of False Worship through Sexual Sin

To put it simply, sexual sin was a high place of self-worship and demon worship in the Old Testament. So-called *worshippers* would climb up on the altar and offer sexual acts, among other things, as worship to a demon god. Remember, God commanded His people to destroy any high places remaining in the lands they took from the Canaanites when Joshua began the full invasion of their promised land. Instead, not only did the generations following Joshua fail to do that, King Solomon, in disappointing fashion, erected brand new high places for demon gods. *Remember, we're not talking about the heathen Gentile world here.* These are God's chosen people engaged in the high places of sexual sin.

High Places Created a Defiling Influence

A very interesting fact is that these high places influenced the entire nation to sin. The sins tolerated or committed personally by the king on the high place were not isolated to them as individuals. Their actions had extraordinary corporate repercussions on the nation they ruled, in which the high places remained. It's as if these tolerated high places cast some kind of spell over the tribes of Israel and influenced them in a sinful way.

I have personally been to Israel and stood on some of these high places. Jezebel, wife of Ahab, housed herself on some of these high places to offer her false worship. Two of them were Mt. Megiddo and Mt. Carmel. The views from these high places are truly extraordinary as the expanse of the valleys of Israel is clearly seen below. I could then imagine how false worship from these high places could have released a shadowy spell over the valleys and nation the same way smoke from an intense fire would billow over the valleys. In a spiritual and evil sense, that's what happened in those Old Testament days.

There is an interesting figure in the history of the kings of Israel, Jeroboam the son of Nebat. God installed him as king over Israel after the Lord separated the two kingdoms as a result of Solomon's sins. However, Jeroboam didn't follow after the Lord. Instead, he, too, set up high places of false worship. Solomon built several in the territory of Judah but now Jeroboam was going to build many throughout the whole land of Israel. Please pay attention: because of his own personal sins in setting up the high places, the Bible says of Jeroboam that he *made the entire nation of Israel to sin*. Again, one man influenced the entire nation to sin against God. To make matters much worse the Bible goes on to describe nearly ten kings after him as not having departed from the "*sins of Jeroboam, son of Nebat, who made all Israel to sin.*"

Wow. Can you imagine that? One man of influence, a king, caused an entire nation to sin which then led to many generations of kings to follow in his depravity. Granted, the sins of leaders do not negate one's personal responsibility to follow the Lord wholeheartedly. Nevertheless, the effects of sin through establishing high places of false worship would be staggering and devastating for generations to come. Ultimately, it destroyed the nation.

"[God]…*tore Israel from the house of David, and they made Jeroboam the son of Nebat king. Then* **Jeroboam drove Israel from following the LORD, and made them commit a great sin.** *For the children of Israel walked in all the sins of Jeroboam which he did; they did not depart from them.*" (2 Kings 17:21-22)

Not good; yet it's very clear. In a very practical and telling way the individual people of Israel and Judah had a lot of help in their sinning against the Lord. The high places of demon worship cast a prevailing evil over the people of God and it pressured them to sin, too. How interesting is that?

Have you ever felt like you had help in sinning from an influence you couldn't see? Many of us have walked into an environment where there was a powerful and unusual sense of sexual uncleanness. All of the sudden your mind might become flooded with impure sexual thoughts and not really understand why. If you're a guy like me, maybe all you thought was, "Man, I feel like I want to fornicate with every female in this room! What the heck is going on?!" Well, what happened? Are you some kind of evil, loathsome whore or whoremonger? Of course not. It's very possible that you just entered a sexually unclean environment.

Maybe someone in that group opened a door to the demonic through sin and you're picking up on the funkiness. You might be tempted to feel like you're the one with the problem but it may be that the lust and defilement on someone else in that vicinity is being projected onto you making you feel like something you're not.

Obviously you want to get out of that environment or that person's presence as quickly as possible. Then deal with any potential effects the environment may have had on you promptly and Biblically. However, the point, and to bring this into context, is that these idolatrous Old Testament high places had this type of destructive influence on an entire region. No wonder God spoke to His people to utterly destroy all of these false altars of worship.

High Places were Generational

Not only did high places create a defiling influence they were also generational. A significant and sad fact is that the high places of worship remained in Judah, Israel's counterpart even longer. They stood for nearly 300 years. For over a dozen generations Judah's kings failed to obey God's command to go up and completely destroy these high places and loose the people from the defiling influences. Although *some* of these kings were very godly (unlike *all* of the wicked kings of Israel), the Bible repeatedly states that they, "...*did what was right in the sight of the Lord as his father David.* **Nevertheless the high places of worship were not removed.**"

Here is what we need to see: there was genuine worship coming from God's people Judah, while there was also great compromise. Both were going on at the same time. Again, during the reign of some great kings, like Asa, Jehoshaphat and Hezekiah, the worship of the God of Israel was faithfully offered from the temple at Jerusalem. Yet these other altars of false worship were tolerated and allowed to remain. This godly nation was still held captive in many ways.

New Testament Strongholds

For the weapons of our warfare are not carnal but mighty in God for **pulling down strongholds, casting down arguments and every high thing** *that exalts itself against the knowledge of God, bringing every thought into captivity to the obedience of Christ, and being ready to punish all disobedience when your obedience is fulfilled.* (2 Corinthians 10:4-6)

There is a striking parallel between what the Old Testament calls *high places* and what the New Testament calls *strongholds*. The passage above and the one in Deuteronomy share phenomenal similarities.

Let's first consider their differences. High places point primarily to an outward influence while strongholds refer primarily to an inward influence. The Old Testament high places were literal, physical places of worship. New Testament strongholds are sins of the mind. High places were obviously high in natural elevation while strongholds are high in rank and influence in the soul. Old Testament high places affected a nation. A New Testament stronghold affects the person. High places represent worship to a demon god. A stronghold represents submission to a lie thus preventing the Lord from being fully worshipped through the believer. Since a stronghold represents believing and living according to a lie, it can therefore be arguably interpreted as indirect worship to the father of lies. It's a stretch but I think we understand the point.

Strongholds are basically any bit of concocted information in our brain that opposes and challenges the Word of God. They are strong arguments and reasoning that hold sway in our thought lives. They are not merely the thinking of a bad thought. Strongholds are persuasive lies, deceptive theories, twisted truth, misguided ideas, convincing or believable untruths in the soul life. This gives rise to the battlefield of the mind.

Caroline Leaf, Ph.D., has an extensive resume of experience when it comes to the science of thought. In her book, *Who Switched Off My Brain?*, she noted that, *"thoughts are measurable and occupy mental 'real estate.'"*1 It then makes perfect sense why we're told not to give ground or place to the devil in our thought life. An interesting note is that a stronghold is defined in the Greek language as a *castle*. The only problem is that King Jesus isn't living there! God needs to be living in the real estate of our soul.

Similarities of High Places and Strongholds

Let's now see some similarities between high places in the Old Testament with that of strongholds in the New Testament.

First: They both prevent God from being fully worshipped by His people, whether by nation or by individual.

Second: They both have tremendous influence. One leads a nation to sin and the other leads the individual believer to sin.

Third: Sexual sin was a high place of worship among God's Holy nation of Israel and is now a stronghold within His Church. Sexual compromise is widely accepted and exercised in the Body of Christ.

Fourth: Both are generational. We already saw this played out in Old Testament examples. Kind David had sex with a married woman. Later his son Amnon became distressed by a sexually unclean spirit. He fell in love with his half-sister and raped her (2 Samuel 13). Immediately after the incident Amnon intensely hated her and rejected her. In today's times, you don't have to look hard to recognize a pattern or generational stronghold of sin in a family line. Many men generationally deal with strongholds of rejection, father wounds, alcoholism, pornography and anger. Many women are faced with generational strongholds of mistrust of men, children out of wedlock, fear and depression. High places and strongholds seemed to be passed down from one generation to the next, including sexual sin.

Fifth: They were both commanded by God to be smashed. High places were to be torn down and physically destroyed. Strongholds are to be cast down and demolished by our spiritual weapons of warfare.

The Stronghold of Sexual Immorality

Many young Christians are losing to sexual sin. They live sexually active and are thus bound by a stronghold. Others are bound, not necessarily by any acts of sexual sin, but by lies concerning sex. You can be living sex free but bound nonetheless through strongholds and lies. Believing these lies can and will lead many into sexual sin. That's one reason why strongholds or high places in the mind need to be brought down. The sooner the better. If young believers are taught right to begin with, then the strongholds would probably not be as firmly established in the first place.

Let's identify some of the more basic lies, fortified arguments or strongholds in the minds of young adults concerning sex:

- *Nobody is living right.*
- *I'm the only one trying to do what's right.*
- *It's not possible to live with sexual integrity.*
- *God really doesn't expect me to live with sexual integrity.*
- *God understands if or when I compromise sexually considering the culture I live in.*
- *God will forgive me for having sex before marriage (true) so it really doesn't matter anyways (false).*
- *Sexual activity or giving away my virginity is not really a big deal.*
- *Obedience in this area will equal misery.*
- *I can never live with self-control in this area.*
- *Heavy petting, oral sex, manual stimulation to orgasm and masturbation without sexual intercourse isn't sex and is therefore acceptable.*
- *If I choose to live in compromise right now all of the sexually immoral pressures and conflicts due to sexual sin will all go away after I'm married.*

The list goes on. The huge truth here is that where these strongholds exist there will be an outward expression of that inward belief. Dr. Leaf went on to write, "*Thoughts influence every decision, word, action, and physical reaction we make.*"[2] In other words, a person will live out what they believe.

As a man "*thinks in his heart so is he.*" (Proverbs 23:7)

Jesus said in Matthew 15:19 that, "*out of the heart proceed evil thoughts...adulteries, fornications.*" Again, just as the high places influenced a nation to sin so a stronghold leads a Christian to sin. If you think that nobody is living right then you'll be a bitter and critical Christian. Elijah had this mindset for a while and it caused him to want to die and to think all kinds of weird things (1 Kings

19:1-18). If you don't think there are people out there living right, then it won't be long before you won't be living right, too. If you don't think it's possible to live with sexual integrity or God doesn't really expect you to, then you won't either. If you don't think blowing your virginity is a big deal then you will. If you think that you cannot live with self-control, then you won't. This is why strongholds must be demolished. Good or bad a Christian will live what he or she believes.

Let me share with you a personal testimony of how some strongholds concerning premarital sex were brought down in my life.

My Genuine Turning Point

Earlier in chapter two I mentioned the "Why Wait" seminar my dad made me and my sister attend. The testimony of the speaker, which I am about to share, had a profound effect on me. As I already said I went in to this seminar a somewhat resentful Christian. I was personally disappointed that it seemed like few peer aged Christians were living sexually holy. I also felt like God was letting them get away with it.

I had turned into the prodigal's brother and felt like I understood his misplaced resentment. Unfortunately, there weren't a lot of fathers, mentors or leaders around that ministered to guys like me in a way that the father did in the parable. I was also upset that it seemed like all my sisters in Christ, who knew better, were living in compromise, too. It was as if I felt abandoned by my own. I understood the passage where some of God's people bitterly said in Malachi 3:14-15:

> *"It is useless to serve God; what profit is it that we have kept His ordinance, and that we have walked...before the Lord of Hosts? So now we call the proud blessed, for those who do wickedness are raised up; they even tempt God and go free."*

Take a guess at what this line of thinking this was? A stronghold indeed! I needed some cheese with my whine! I was beginning to believe some major lies and was fighting acting out on those lies by becoming a fornicating fool due to bitterness.

In the book *Boundaries*, Doctors Cloud and Townsend speak about the person caught up in this kind of confused envy, noting "*a person chooses the righteous life, but envies and resents those who seem to be 'having all the fun'.*" They went on to write that "*your envy should always be a sign to you that you are lacking something.*"[3] How true. These kinds of slowly surfacing wounds in me were pointing to a deeper issue of insecurity, rejection, feelings of abandonment and fear. Thankfully, God was positioning me in order to set me free through this God encounter.

The thirty something speaker begins the packed out seminar by sharing his own personal testimony. He was raised in church and hit his teen years. He had a ton of questions for God and his most agitating one had to do with sex. He liked girls. He liked the idea of sex. He wanted to have some sex. However he was really trying to stay a virgin. Obviously he knew the Scriptures about waiting but in his mind he needed more clarity. However, his frustrations grew because he felt ignored by God and his questions went seemingly left unanswered. Eventually, this festered into resentment and offense toward God. He ultimately acted out on his anger and it led him to have sex with a girl from his church in a car in the church parking lot.

Well, right about here this guy had my attention. He went on to share that from this single experience he spiraled into years of sexual craziness, plus all the bitterness multiplied. Then something interesting happened. He went on one date with a particular girl. He was attempting to touch her sexually and she instantly quoted aloud a Bible Scripture. He stopped, startled. She continued to say that the reason she chose to go out on a date with him is because she heard that he was a Christian and then voiced her disappointment. Ouch! Talk about a reality check.

Fast forward many years: he eventually wholeheartedly sought restoration with the Lord. God began a most awesome work of healing and redemption in his life. It was during this time he began dating a Christian girl which brought about the redemptive side of his testimony. They were together for seven years and both thought they were meant by God to be married to each other. Get this: during these seven years this guy not only doesn't have sex with her, but he never even touched her.

Well, as it turned out they did not get married after all. There was a mutually consented break-up as they both eventually sensed God had another plan for them separate from one another. He was hurt by their God-ordained-break-up but wanted with all of his heart the Lord's best for her and of course for him.

Eventually God brought to this woman the right man to be her husband. The bride to be invites her ex-boyfriend of seven years, the speaker of this seminar, to her wedding. After the ceremony the new bride introduces for the first time her ex-boyfriend of seven years to her new husband. While in her wedding dress she tells her new husband of her ex-boyfriend, as they were all together, *"This is the man who made me the person I am today."*

Ay caramba! After hearing this I practically had to be peeled off the floor and needed an entire box of Kleenex. To this day the new bride's statement describing this man still touches my heart. You see, after all of his pain and failure, God transformed this brother and proved him to be a real man of honor and integrity. He allowed the Lord to do a true work of redemption in his own life, heal his bitterness and empower him to obey concerning sexual purity.

As a result this guy became a real hero. He did it right. He was the example of Christ to his girlfriend of seven years. He protected and covered her by not taking advantage of her. He laid down his own life, crucified his sin nature and eventually presented her pure and chaste for another man to marry. Sexual integrity is not about being perfect. It is about becoming willing, wherever you are in your walk, to let God have all of your heart and body. It is about dying to your own plans and empowering God to resurrect you at His appointed time.

Because of his anointed testimony I knew right then that I could live right. He did it right and it penetrated every part of my thinking. By God's grace my new brother in Christ helped tear down a stronghold in my life. I had a stinking liar talking in my ear for a long time. But at that point I knew it was possible to wait to have sex until I was married. I now had a vision. I wanted to be a hero for some young girl just like this guy was. Sure, I still wanted sex but my motivations began to change. I wanted to do things God's way and pursue His highest and best. I began to believe that the cost would not compare to the value of the final product; first, honoring the One who created me; second, being married and having all the legal sex I want for the rest of my life. All of this and being smack in the will of God? It sounded good to me.

Again, in Christlike fashion, this guy selflessly laid down his life for that young woman. God always has a hero, like this man was for me. Now, we see one who, in Bible history, finally takes down the high places of the Old Testament in dramatic fashion and prophetic passion.

Going Up to the High Places

A young boy comes on the scene in Judah's history by the name of Josiah. He becomes king at the age of eight. His grandfather Manasseh was the worst and longest reigning of all the kings in Judah. His father Amon lasted as king for only two years because of his wickedness. Yet, in a dramatic and remarkable prophecy some three hundred years before his birth, an unknown prophet declares that a child by the name of Josiah would reign as king. He declared that Josiah would overthrow the false priests of the high places and even burn their bones on that same altar (1 Kings 13:1-2). Nearly 300 years later in 2 Chronicles 34 we see him do that and much more. What so many other good and godly kings failed to do, Josiah followed through and accomplished.

> "*Josiah was eight years old when he became king, and he reigned thirty-one years in Jerusalem. And* **he did what was right in the sight of the LORD,** *and walked in the ways of his father David; he did not*

46

turn aside to the right hand or to the left. For in the eighth year of his reign, while he was still young, he began to seek the God of his father David; and in the twelfth year he began to purge Judah and Jerusalem of the high places, the wooden images, the carved images, and the molded images. **They broke down the altars of the Baals in his presence, and the incense altars which were above them he cut down; and the wooden images, the carved images, and the molded images he broke in pieces, and made dust of them and scattered it on the graves of those who had sacrificed to them. He also burned the bones of the priests on their altars, and cleansed Judah and Jerusalem.** *And so he did in the cities of Manasseh, Ephraim, and Simeon, as far as Naphtali and all around, with axes. When he had broken down the altars and the wooden images, had beaten the carved images into powder, and cut down all the incense altars throughout all the land of Israel, he returned to Jerusalem.*" (2 Chronicles 34:1-7)

Another awesome fact was that not only were the high places totally destroyed but even the bones of the false prophets were burned. This can be likened to the Lord not only removing our sin but also the reproach of the sin. None of us want to feel guilty, condemned or depressed over sin. It's as though God is giving a preview of His redemptive plan and the blood of Christ purging our conscience of the sin, and thus, removing the toxic and lingering effects (Hebrews 9:14). Not only is the sin forgiven but the stain of sin removed.

Under Josiah's leadership the high places were destroyed. The nation served God fully all of his days. Just as disobedience had a defiling influence over the nation, now through obedience, blessing and God's presence affected the nation. God always was and is so very redemptive!

Jeroboam may have messed stuff up but Josiah took care of business. Adam may have messed things up but Jesus Christ turned it around for you and me!

"Here it is in a nutshell: Just as one person did it wrong and got us in all this trouble with sin and death, another person did it right and got us out of it. But more than just getting us out of trouble, he got us into life! One man said no to God and put many people in the wrong; one man said yes to God and put many people in the right." (Romans 5:18-19, MESSAGE)

You might look around and think, "Will someone please rise up and do what's right and lead by example?!" Know for sure that God always raises up some young person to go up to the high places of sin and bring them down! You are called to be one of them.

Who Said?

Let's go up to these high places. Challenge and smash the status quo. Who said you cannot be a virgin when you get married? Who said you couldn't live a holy life from this moment forward? Who said there aren't any stud young men of God out there? Who said God doesn't have any young women who are giving themselves wholly to the Lord? Who said there are not any captivating and resourceful women like Rebekah, who was beautiful in form and appearance? Who said every Christian is out there having sex? Who said you can't discipline your body? Who said you'll never meet the right one? Who said it would be better to just have sex and repent later? Who said God doesn't know best? Who said God isn't paying attention to you and so you have to watch out for yourself? Who said God doesn't pay big for obedience? Real truth is what comes from the mouth of the Lord.

"Let God be true and every man be a liar." (Romans 3:4)

Choose to believe God's report. Let's pray according to the Truth and may the Holy Spirit wield His Sword right into any strongholds in your mind and bring lasting freedom:

PRAYER:

"Heavenly Father, I want Your very best for my life. I desire to live in a way that pleases, honors and glorifies You. I don't want to live in sexual compromise. I choose life and blessing. Help me and teach me to pull down the strongholds in my life that are preventing me from living in Your Life-giving Truth. May every argument, imagination and reasoning in my mind that is opposing Your Word be pulled down and smashed. If in any way I have aligned myself with lies of the enemy or have come into agreement with the compromise of this culture, I repent of it now. I renounce and reject them. Teach me to wield my weapons of warfare. This moment I use the name of Jesus, the Word of God and appropriate the power of the blood of Jesus to cleanse my conscience from every evil work so I can fully serve the living God, according to the Hebrews 9:14. I thank you for it all. I receive Your love, forgiveness, healing and confidence in Jesus name, amen!"

Chapter 6

Restoring Innocence
What to Do If You're Already a Mess

I f you're reading this thinking that you're nowhere close to where you should be concerning sexual integrity, then hopefully this chapter can help guide you forward. You might be a thousand miles off course and feel like you have little self-will when it comes to standing against sexual temptation. Maybe you've liked this book, but in all truth, you may be so far into sin that you feel the first five chapters were too little, too late. However, if it's your heart's cry to get back on track with God in this area of your life, then He will absolutely make a way. If you are in this place right now and desire restoration, then this chapter is for you.

It appears that the process of true Biblical restoration follows a somewhat consistent Scriptural pattern. Please understand this chapter is more basic in principle and not in any way an exhaustive study of becoming healed or cleansed of sexual sin or trauma. Thankfully there are many wonderful books and ministries with that calling and grace. However, this is not a deliverance manual or a deep inner healing discipleship course. Rather the following are simply core principles that should be woven into any instruction on restoration and practiced regardless. Thankfully from here the Holy Spirit can do a wonderful and powerful work in you as He knows your heart to draw near to Him.

Anytime a Christian gets caught up in a tailspin of iniquity, rebellion or a habitual prodigal lifestyle, the Restorer then always works to create a plan of rescue. He did that when man first sinned and still does it for us today.

51

Remember that God delights in mercy. Although the choice for restoration is ours, it is always His heart's desire to see His lost sons return back to the Father's house and restored fully into Sonship. Let's use the familiar story found in Luke 15 of the prodigal son and his father, a type of our Heavenly Father, as a pattern for true restoration.

It Stinks to Be Me Right Now!

Let's start with the desperation this guy is in. The prodigal's mounted sins are no lightweight matter whatsoever. First, he wants his portion of inheritance before his dad passes away. Although Jewish law allowed a father to abdicate his wealth prior to his death (1 Kings 1:2), the attitude from the son to the father is almost as such, "I wish you were dead!" Hatred can not only lead to murder but is the same as murder.

You may have felt similarly if you had a bad father but this young man was blessed with an All-Star of a dad. This younger son's request also betrayed his rebellious nature in wanting to live independently of his father's will. He then leaves the divine connection of his family and heads for a foreign land. He wastes his money and willfully messes himself up with immoral women. This is where he gets knocked out because following his immorality, the son adds apostasy. He joins himself to a gentile farmer who raises pigs, which were regarded in the Jewish faith as unclean. This marks a clear departing from his spiritual faith of a beautifully rich Jewish heritage as he makes a covenant with a foreigner.

The young man's rebellion can be summarized in wrecking his family, wasting his wealth, embracing adultery and violating the covenant of his God. This is well beyond making some mistakes. This is a willful defiance of God and a lifestyle of iniquity. Unfortunately, rebellion always leads to poverty of soul and oftentimes of substance. Yet from this pit we find the potential seed for genuine change.

CHAPTER 6

Measurable Process of Restoration

*"But when **he came to himself**, he said, 'How many of my father's hired servants have bread enough and to spare, and I perish with hunger!'" (Luke 15:17-18)*

Revelation: At his worst condition the Bible says that the young man *"came to himself."* This can be defined as a moment of revelation in his life including choices, their consequences and his circumstances. In a flash he receives heaven's perspective concerning his world. It's as if the lights turned on in his hazy head and he saw his life in one sane and clear moment.

First, there is a remarkable and touching fact of how the father is present in the son's memory while in that far country. We can see then that revelation often starts with the remembrance of the Lord and His goodness. Secondly, the young man says to himself, "What am I doing here? Why am I living like this? What have I become? Why am I eating pigs' food?" Revelation can lead us to a raw reality of a degrading condition. This normally leaves a person feeling disgusted with themselves and recognizing the desperate need for a life change. At this point we can also feel very alone and ashamed.

This *"coming to himself"* moment shed light on his impoverished circumstances of body and soul. This was more than a gut check or a convicted conscience. This guy's conscience was already seared and he was more than likely close to natural death. This is why this revelation experience is no ordinary thing. It is a genuine moment of truth inspired of love. For any person to enjoy restoration there is often first this same "lights on" experience. It was in this moment the prodigal was allowed the opportunity to become contrite and therefore given the opportunity to make the appropriate changes.

How are these moments of revelation generated? For one, *pain brings perspective.* Tough doses of reality bring about a rare sobriety in one's heart. It's sort of like being at a wedding or a funeral. Our perspective becomes enlarged and clearer as we reflect on our own lives and decisions. It feels terribly humiliating to be at an all-time low in life and living with the pigs when we're meant for so much more. The passing pleasure of sin will turn on us and leave us a frustrated prisoner. At this point there is really nowhere else to look but up. It is from this place of pain and perspective that we find true Micah 7:8, *"When I sit in darkness the Lord will be a light unto me."*

From our self-imposed pit God faithfully gives us a supernatural remembrance of Himself and His goodness. What we do with this revelation is our choice but we would be unable to change without it and thus perish in that foreign land (Proverbs 29:18) to where our sin drove us. Know this: God is Light and is seeking opportunities to bring His rescuing illumination to us the way He did for this young man. God's heart is not to embarrass us by turning on the lights. He wants to help us.

My senior year in high school I made a last second, off balance three pointer that put our basketball team into the Division II CIF finals. The crowds went nuts, the cheer leaders cheered and it was all over the paper the next day. If you're ever at my home more than a few times, you will be forced to watch the video. I will then be transformed into the late Chick Hearns as I announce the final minute play by play. For those too unspiritual not to be a Lakers fan, Chickie is the hall-of-fame announcer for the Lakers from the early sixties all the way to the Shaq and Kobe dynasty. Anyhow, I'm not as bad as Uncle Rico from *Napoleon Dynamite,* but pretty close. When I was interviewed by the newspaper following the game I did what any good Christian would do and gave some props to the Lord. All kidding aside, I genuinely wanted to honor the Lord as the shot was so bizarre that it seemed like there was some angelic guidance to get that ball into the net.

Well, three days later we lost the championship game in the final six seconds to a team that went into the playoffs with a losing record. It was very sucky and very painful. Guys hate to lose. Well, following that championship loss, a Christian friend's father came up and put his arm around me and said, "Sam, I know it hurts but you've acknowledged the Lord and that's what's most important." At the time I didn't feel all that comforted but that experience would come back as a moment of revelation in my life.

About a year later I was really struggling in my relationship with the Lord and in a major conflict as to what direction I was going to choose for my future: was I going to serve God with my whole heart or not? Well, it seemed like I was beginning to choose the wrong direction. I started going to parties with my friends. I was the most pathetic wannabe you've ever seen. I was trying to fit into the scene but was like a fish out of water. I felt like Lloyd Christmas from *Dumb and Dumber* "sitting by the bar, putting out the vibe". I desperately needed a moment of revelation from God and thankfully He came through.

One night while walking down a street as we were headed toward a party, I looked to my right and saw in the front lawn of a nearby home the same man who encouraged me in God after we lost that championship game. He was looking right at me. We both knew where I was headed. It startled me and the lights turned on. I didn't see any condemnation in his eyes as he watched me walk toward this non-Chuckie Cheese bash. God didn't send Jesus to condemn any of us (John 3:17). But it was as if the Lord was allowing me to see that I was straying; that others were aware of my testimony and were closely watching my decisions of lifestyle; and that He loved me and wanted to give me the opportunity to turn around. It was both sobering and a little embarrassing.

Shortly after this experience I walked into another party and one of my skater neighbors was there. He walked right up to me and looked me in the face and said, "What are *you* doing here?" It was as if God Himself said it. How faithful God was to give me another huge moment of revelation during my valley of decision. I stopped in my tracks startled again. I looked at him and said, "I don't know!" I turned around and immediately drove home and have never been to a drinking party from that moment until now. We all need those moments of revelation and God is always so faithful to bring them when our hearts are ready. I'm so thankful. The young man who said that to me has spent a lot of years in prison. That could have been me.

Many times the light hasn't yet turned on for a rebellious person because God knows their heart. Perhaps they will not respond with obedience and, therefore, He will wait rather than make them responsible and accountable to a moment of truth.

> Isaiah 30:18 says, *"Therefore the LORD will wait, that He may be gracious to you; And therefore He will be exalted, that He may have mercy on you. For the LORD is a God of justice; Blessed are all those who wait for Him."*

There is a precious time when your heart is more vulnerable and tender and God is willing to wait for that time. God wants to vindicate you from evil that is trying to draw you away from Him. Revelation helps you to see evil as it really is and therefore make you zealously see that you're nobody's slave but God's. If, however, that revelation comes too soon then it could be more harmful than destructive.

> Jesus said, *"To whom much is given from him much will be required."* (Luke 12:48)

Therefore, it is good to ask the Lord in prayer, over ourselves and others, for a teachable heart. This can afford us the opportunity to hopefully respond with tenderness and repentance. An effective Bible prayer is that God would grant us all repentance that we *"may know the truth, and that they may come to their senses and escape the snare of the devil, having been taken captive by him to do his will"* (2 Timothy 2:25-26).

Revelation affords us the opportunity to take the next step in this process of restoration called *repentance*.

CHAPTER 6

Repentance:

> *"I will arise and go to my father, and will say to him, 'Father, I have sinned against heaven and before you, and I am no longer worthy to be called your son. Make me like one of your hired servants.' And he arose and came to his father."* (Luke 15:18-20)

The obvious right move after being illuminated to a wavering condition would be to repent for missing the mark. There are several components to this second step we can safely see in this story:

Sorrow for Sin: Contriteness marks repentance. It's simple. You should be genuinely sorry for what you've done in sinning against the Lord or others. Not this business of, "I'm sorry if what I did hurt you." Whatever. Our heart should be, "I am very sorry for what I've done and the hurt I've caused."

There are all kinds of ungodly sorrow out there in the world that Jesus already carried on the Cross (Isaiah 53). Let's resists those. However, there is a godly sorrow as well. When embraced, this godly sorrow produces repentance.

> 2 Corinthians 7:10 says that *"...godly grief and the pain God is permitted to direct, produce a repentance that leads and contributes to salvation and deliverance from evil, and it never brings regret."* (AMP)

God doesn't produce the grief. Our own sin does that.

> *"Now the mind of the flesh [which is sense and reason without the Holy Spirit] is death [death that comprises **all the miseries arising from sin**, both here and hereafter]."* (Romans 8:6, AMP)

Misery arises from sin and not from God. However since God is always bigger He can even direct miseries and pain for good, with no side effects of regret. There is a brokenness and contriteness of spirit that is acceptable to God (Psalm 51:17) that can *lead* us toward repentance. Please do not confuse this with a self-depreciating and unbiblical idea that you're worthless. You cannot be worthless and worth the Blood of Christ at the same time. You are a new creation in Christ that was led astray by the lusts of your own flesh and are now experiencing healthy pain.

In his devotional book, *Who I Am in Christ*, Dr. Neil Anderson wrote:

> *"Repeated defeats in the life of Christians are capitalized by Satan. He pours on guilt, and coupled with the negative influence of legalistic teachers, Christians often question their salvation or accept as normal an up-and-down spiritual existence. They confess their wretchedness and proneness to sin and strive to do better, but inwardly they consider themselves only as sinners saved by grace, hanging on until the rapture. Why does this happen to so many Christians? Because of ignorance of our true identity in Christ. Praise God, we are no longer just a product of our past. 'Therefore, if anyone is in Christ he is a new creation, the old has gone, the new has come!' (2 Corinthians 5:17) When you see yourself as God sees you, as His child and a saint, it becomes a joy to cooperate with Him in His transforming work in your life."[1]*

Be encouraged you that your sin has not altered your value or identity. You are greatly loved and valued by God and sin did not change that.

A few thoughts:

FIRST: The prodigal was pained for what he did, not flippant or arrogant. Please notice, the prodigal didn't come home and tell everybody to "get over it." He didn't say, "*Hey, it's in the past. You guys are all so ultra-sensitive. Quit taking everything so personal. It ain't about you. Oh well, it's only money. After all, the loose women I was with were pretty hot! Let me show you pictures of all of my girlfriends while I was out there. I'm hungry! Are the lamb chops ready? Yo, slave, rub my feet! It was a flippin' long walk home!*" I don't think so. This kind of attitude does not reflect genuine godly sorrow.

Remember, sexual sin produces pride and gives off a stench of arrogance within one's personality. Sexual sin also hurts others. There may still be some people a little sensitive about your past conduct. They may need some healing too. You're not their healer but an attitude of humility can sure help.

SECOND: Discern the difference between healthy conviction over sin versus condemnation and shame. Shame makes you *run away from* God and His people rather than *run to* God and His people. The prodigal *went back* to his father's house and his family, *not from* them. Therefore we can clearly see that godly sorrow, not condemnation, was drawing him to repentance. These toxic influences of condemnation and shame are not our motivations for repentance nor are they God inspired.

THIRD: The goodness of God also leads us to repentance (Romans 2:4). The son had a 'good memory' of his father's house and it helped lead him to change. Both of these positive forces, godly sorrow and the goodness of God were at work within this young brother to produce true repentance and ultimately got him back home. They will be at work to get any of us back home too.

Confession of Sin: From your heart, and out of your mouth, is to be the plain confession of sin. "I did this. It was my fault. I am the man. The devil didn't make me do it. This is what I did and it was wrong and I ask for your forgiveness." This is simple, but necessary.

> 1 John 1:9 says, "*If we confess our sins, **He is faithful** and just to forgive us our sins and to cleanse us from all unrighteousness.*"

Some thoughts:

FIRST: True repentance takes ownership. James 1:14 says that "*each one is tempted when he is drawn away by his own desires and enticed.*" Without the authentic confession of sin it is much easier to get dragged back into the sin. Pride tries to prevent us from taking ownership of sin, but the sooner we call it like it is, the sooner we can move on.

SECOND: Confess your sin to God and a trustworthy Christian.

> *"Confess to one another therefore your faults (your slips, your false steps, your offenses, your sins) and pray [also] for one another, that you may be healed and restored [to a spiritual tone of mind and heart]."* (James 5:16, AMP)

Did you notice that you are to confess to God in 1 John 1:9 and confess to "one another" in the James passage? They're both important and necessary. The prodigal confessed to himself, to heaven and to his father. A trusted mentor, pastor, and/or friend are wonderful gifts from God and a possible confidant to whom you can confide.

THIRD: True repentance is sincere and has a right priority. Some people are sorry because they got caught. However, the prodigal was repentant because He sinned not because he ran out of money or because his way was proven wrong. He said, *"I have sinned against heaven."* David said, *"Against You, You only, have I sinned, and done this evil in your sight"* (Psalm 51:4). Genuine confession of sin is genuinely necessary.

Change of Heart:

> *"I will arise and go to my father, and will say to him, 'Father, I have sinned against heaven and before you, and I am no longer worthy to be called your son. Make me like one of your hired servants.'"* (Luke 15:18-19)

This dialogue and change all took place in his heart. Heart change precedes outward change. The guy had a talk with himself. He had a plan. He thought it through. He was going to change some things. Certainly he was partially motivated by need but so what? We are commanded to not forget all of His benefits (Psalm 103), including satisfying our mouths with good things like food. This is where the prodigal was: HUNGRY and in need! But now, things were changing on the inside. He was looking for more than filling His belly. He was looking to go back home. We prosper in our lives only as we first prosper in our heart and soul (3 John 2).

Change of Action: The prodigal went home: "*and he arose and came to his father* (verse 20)." Eventually repentance shows itself in actions, behavior and conduct. For you this means sexual activity should cease. If you are sexually active then a change of action for you would be to stop having sex. Furthermore, if you are active in the dating scene and by the third date with the same person the heavy petting and sexual foreplay begins, then your change of action will be to stop dating. Your change of action wouldn't be expressed necessarily through a stronger sense of self-will on the third date. Your specific change of action might be to avoid the first date entirely for a while.

The enemy will attempt to pressure your flesh to get you back into the dating scene again. By "the dating scene," I'm referring dating just because it's fun and it's the thing to do. He will continue to test you in your areas of past compromise until he is sure you are no longer caving in over a consistent period of time. He has limited resources.

I remember my youth pastor telling me a story when I was in my early teens. He knew of a guy who would get in bed with a random girl and have sex. He would then immediately face the bedroom wall and confess 1 John 1:9. Yes, he would ask for forgiveness but is that true repentance marked by change of action? Change of action is visible obedience. It is the fruit and outward manifestation of a heart that has been changed. Thankfully, it is also that part of our obedience that purifies our soul from the disobedience we've been in.

Let's change our actions by going home and staying home because *repentance* will bring us to *reinstatement*.

Reinstatement:

"*When he was still a great way off, his father saw him and had compassion, and ran and fell on his neck and kissed him…But the father said to his servants, 'Bring out the best robe and put it on him, and put a ring on his hand and sandals on his feet.'"* (Luke 15:20, 22-23)

This portion of the restoration process is not intended to be a thorough study on what the robe, ring and sandals represent. However it doesn't take long to see their significance. He is reinstated back into Sonship. He is forgiven, valued, covered, and provided for, and he has true identity once again. He has recovered what has been lost. This is one of the great redemptive facets of restoration. Although the son disavowed his covenant with God and father by leaving and making a covenant with the gentile, the father never disowned his son. Now the son, who once threw off his true identity, is now reinstated by his return. He is not a servant but a son.

How much healing must have taken place as the son fully received his father's embrace and affection. Relationships, as God created them, are not transactional or rigid but in fact *relational*. This includes feelings of affection and emotions of compassion. Although the son chose to no longer welcome his father's love, the father never stopped loving the son. Anyone can choose to keep the door of their heart shut to God's love. However, we cannot even love until we first receive His love. Allowing ourselves to be loved after we have sinned can be difficult but we must learn to receive.

Sin turns us all into slaves. It is not our true place of value or identity. But in our return through repentance, we see here the Lord doing what only He can do. We do nothing here, but simply receive His goodness, embrace and reinstatement. Here we are not only in a familiar and safe place; we are home, in our right place.

Rejoicing:

Rejoicing includes your being celebrated by others through your return and your personal celebration through your return. This can be "mucho" hard to do though. Most in this process are caught up in the regret and disappointment of their failures. Although we must try to always remember the lessons, we also must *forget* the reproach.

God intends for His grace to abound where sin once abounded in your life. God's mercy is victorious over judgment. Weeping through godly sorrow may endure for a night but joy over restoration comes in the morning. God intends to remove the stains of reproach, embarrassment and defilement of sin, and the lack of confidence due to past rebellion. With that said we are glad heaven is thrilled over the one that repents but what do we do when we feel unworthy or humiliated over the mistakes we've made?

Allow yourself to be rejoiced over and celebrated by the Father. You were made for this and God's mercy and restoration is the perfect answer for that need. Remember: in the Father's House or in His Presence there is fullness of joy (Psalm 16:11). Fullness of joy implies the absence of the other ugly emotions you feel due to sin.

After choosing to rise up and serve God with all of my heart following my crossroads experience, I remember sitting at home on Friday nights reading my Bible. I had just quit going to parties and now this 18 year old single guy was sitting in a recliner reading a Bible! I cannot fully explain it but I felt so much joy and exhilaration, it was beyond anything I had ever experienced. I could literally feel God's joy inside of me. It was as if my being there made God happy and I could feel His happiness. His joy made me glad.

I was also extra happy just to be happy. Like many of you I had read the Scriptures about His joy since I was a kid but now I was beginning to person-ally experience it beyond any level I had before. It was genuinely inexpressible (1 Peter 1:8). God was celebrating me and He somehow let me in on the party. He will do the same for you. It's just something you will have to experience for yourself. This joy was priceless to me and I wouldn't have traded it for a party with all the "hotties" in the world.

Besides that, as I said earlier, I was the most pathetic person that ever attended a party. I looked absolutely ridiculous. I was going nowhere, fast. Here I am, a church boy trying to fit in on the party scene. There's drinking, fornicating and all kinds of craziness going on, and here I am in the middle of it: **not** drinking, **not** fornicating and **not** getting crazy. I was like one of the *Roxbury* guys. I was miserable and making all of my friends miserable. That's what happens when you don't rise up and serve God. You make everybody sick!

I will never forget my friend Steve Hilliard looking at me one night at a party and said, "Why do you do this to yourself?!" God was speaking right through him. Well, God helped me make the turnaround. I was and still am so happy I did. Allow God to celebrate you.

> Zephaniah 3:17 says, *"He will rejoice over you with great gladness. With his love, he will calm all your fears. He will exult over you by singing a happy song."*

He will not sing over you a happy, *working* song, but a happy song. Love is the most powerful force and weapon as it is the only fail proof virtue that will drive out fear in all its forms and manifestations.

As a matter of truth, he was not and nor are you a prodigal any longer. You are a restored son or daughter whose sins have been canceled by the blood of Christ and are now an occasion for testimony of His grace. Allow yourself to be celebrated by your Heavenly Father.

Allow yourself to be rejoiced over and celebrated by God's people. Keep in mind that the father is not the only one at the father's house. The servants were there, as well as other family. When we are moving toward restoration the Lord is not the only one He is restoring us to. The Lord is also restoring us to His family, His people, His Church, His Bride.

Isolation from God-appointed relationships will lead Christians from the Father's house into sin and continued isolation will keep them there. However there is true restoration when the one who was lost is rejoiced over by Christ and the Body of Christ.

Some of us are the worst at receiving anything from people. I was raised with very little so when I met my wife I had a hard time receiving from her family's generosity. This ranged from them paying for my meal to helping me move a piece of furniture. Obviously, I had some fear, pride and insecurity going on. I just had to practice, although with much discomfort, to receive.

Furthermore, perhaps you feel only tolerated by God's people. Remember that God is working on all of us, including the prodigal's brother. So just go ahead and throw yourself a party as long as it's not a pity party. God will be there and His Word promises that He will bring people around you that will cherish, love and rejoice over you for the great things God has done in your life.

Do some rejoicing yourself. God wants His joy to become your joy and for you to rejoice with that joy. This is when you *delight yourself* in the Lord.

I was so happy to be happy as I read my Bible on those Friday nights. One of the sources of my joy was that I began to realize that my inconsistency never changed the Lord's consistency. Malachi 3:6 says, *"For I am the Lord, I do not change; that is why you, O sons of Jacob, are not consumed."* His steadfast covenant love and His unchangeable nature kept me from total destruction. Remember, I used to feel like I was walking on egg shells around the Lord. But I began to learn that my humanity and faults never made God unpredictable. This began to relieve me of a performance mentality, the pressure to impress God by works and the impulse to earn God's approval. God was bigger than me! What a revelation. What a relief. Joy will make it easy to delight yourself in Him and be happy about your new state of full restoration!

PRAYER:

Father, I need to be loved back to You and to Your people. I have headed in the wrong direction and have made a mess of things. I have hurt myself and others through my sin. Like David said in Psalm 51, "I acknowledge my transgressions, and my sin is always before me. Against You, You only have I sinned, and done this evil in Your sight." Thank You for this moment of revelation. I am seeing more clearly what You have intended for me and how I have been off course. I ask for godly sorrow, a change of heart and change of action. I want and choose Your way. I renounce sexual sin, all sexual immorality and every form of sexual uncleanness and my past participation in these things. I want nothing more to do with them or with any sexual sin in Jesus name. Thank you for reinstating me back into full Sonship including all of the benefits. I desire to hear Your songs of joy over me. Heal me where I have been let down by Your people. I receive Your embrace and the embrace of the Body of Christ. I receive Your joy over me and I choose to delight myself in You. In Jesus name, Amen.

Chapter 7

Resisting Sexual Sin – Part One
Practical: Think McFly, Think!

A lrighty then! Let's get down to the nitty-gritty. Sexual sin is a legitimate temptation. The battle against the will of your own flesh is constant. Victories today do not guarantee victories tomorrow. Whatever strongholds are torn down must not be allowed to be rebuilt. Whatever revelation you received in the past to gain ground spiritually must continue to be adhered to or you will again be entangled. You are exhorted to stand against the schemes of the devil and you must walk in the Spirit in order to not fulfill the lusts of the flesh. To put it simply, resisting sexual temptation is nothing short of a serious and ongoing battle. It's all out on the table when you're battling against your human nature. You're in a fight that you should be in and you cannot permit yourself a moment of timidity about it.

Resisting Sexual Sin

Let's get this straight right now. Resisting sexual sin is absolutely do-able. Sure, the percentages are accurate that most young people are sexually active but in no uncertain terms does that mean you have to fall into those numbers or stay in those percentages. No way. Remember, you're not like everybody else. I personally didn't date for three years while waiting for my wife. I didn't do much dating before then either. We got married as virgins. I wasn't touching her breasts or stimulating or penetrating her manually during our 18 month dating and engagement period. There was neither oral sex nor any creative ways to bring one another to orgasm. I have never been involved in any masturbation or pornography in my life. I'm serious. You don't have to go out and live like a monk either. It's a lie that you can't live with sexual integrity and purity. You don't have to know *how* it can be done to be convinced that it *can* be done.

There are a ton of great testimonies out there as some are not even kissing until they tie the knot. People are doing this right and it's helpful for you to know that. Consider this settled: resisting sexual sin is do-able. Believe it. The Bible says that His commandments, including the 'not yet to sex' one, are not burdensome (1 John 5:3). Jesus said that His yoke is easy and His burden is light. God isn't trying to make your life miserable or mess with you. We can and *should know how to possess our own vessels in honor and sanctification*—abstaining from sexual immorality (1 Thessalonians 4:4).

The next two chapters are about the tools God has given you to walk this out with victory. Resisting sexual sin starts way before you find yourself in the backseat of a car with your engine about to overheat. Obviously, this explains why so many people consider sexual purity nearly impossible. Very few of us can step away from those compromising situations. Putting yourself in this situation repeatedly and then miraculously avoiding any sexual sin is like playing with a loaded weapon. It does not make you wise or strong.

Let's now consider some tested Bible ways to resist sexual sin. Yes, we are at that place in the guide where we resist, stand against and say 'no' to sexual sin. As said earlier, you can do this. God has graced you for the test and you have what it takes. God has given you heavenly empowered weapons of warfare as your tools of the trade plus a brain to think with and use. Some of your tools are practical and some seem more spiritual. All are necessary. The following are principles and truths to help you win. In this chapter we'll start with some of the more practical ways we can resist sexual temptation.

CHAPTER 7

FIRST: Use Your Brain to Decrease the Odds of Failure.

"Make no provision for the flesh, to fulfill its lusts." (Romans 13:14)

There are several very practical ways we can help ourselves in this battle. We have no other excuse but to capitalize on these and give ourselves a huge advantage long before a battle begins. These are like free throws in basketball. You gotta make your free throws. Forget about the super spiritual stuff in this chapter. Do the basics and be faithful over what you can control. Be wise and faithful over the natural. There will be plenty of battles later to contend with that seem far beyond your Jedi skills. If you are unfaithful in the natural things then forget about being successful in any realm of spiritual warfare. Be normal and do your part. Don't shoot yourself in the foot. Do the easy stuff. Believe you, me: we need every edge we can get. Simply using our God given brain and making the most basic moral decisions can help us skip a lot of opportunities to be trapped by sin.

We can easily decrease the odds of failure by limiting the number of sexually tempting encounters. A battle avoided is a battle won.

Let's consider a few:

Watch the intake: Jesus says in Matthew 12:33-37 that whatever fruit our lives yield is directly related to the kind of treasure we deposit into our hearts. If we put in the right stuff then we'll eventually produce some good fruit. There will be a positive and godly outflow in our attitude, conversation and habits. Sure, there's more to it, but if you read the passage and check out other corresponding Bible principles then you'll see this important point. Please help yourself and don't be watching any movies that show a man a woman having sex. You're killing yourself. Don't walk into a movie and have no idea of the sexual content. Those experiences, images and sounds are unhealthy deposits into your heart and are without any doubt warring against your soul.

Do not do this at your own personal invitation. You have enough involuntary challenges through commercials, billboards and media. By allowing this we are literally giving our flesh and the devil a ton of free ammunition. We must be wiser. This is not about being religious or legalistic. Also, I'm assuming you're reading this book because you're serious about being proactive to honor God with your body and marry the right person He has for you. So, if you want to excel in sexual integrity then you must use your head.

Primarily what we allow our eyes to see, ears to hear and mouths to speak will become like a deposit of treasure into our hearts, whether good or bad. These three dynamics are like gateways into our hearts. If we are watchful to allow only honorable things to enter into these gateways then as Jesus said, *"Out of the good treasure of his heart brings forth good things."* You have to then really challenge yourself on what it is you're depositing.

Again, if you watch movies where there's sexual activity you are short circuiting your potential for success and messing up your brain. The last thing your soul life needs are these kinds of images imprinted in your mind.

"I will refuse to look at anything vile and vulgar." (Psalm 101:3)

Sex, according to God's original intent, is not vulgar. Watching others have sex is. I would encourage you to purchase a DVD player through a company called ClearPlay. Google them. The player allows for advanced content filtering of DVD's that is nearly seamless in skipping over undesirable content, all in real time. That way you can still enjoy some great movies without any of the bad language and sex scenes. Just tell them to get on the ball and come out with a Blu-ray player.

It will also help to sensitize your conscience if you've grown callous to some of these things. A believer in Jesus Christ is not to receive his or her sex education from movies. That's like eating from the Tree of the Knowledge of Good and Evil. Sin is not your teacher. Sin enslaves you and obscures your perspective.

The Holy Spirit through the Word of God is your teacher. Make the adjustments and He will begin to re-sensitize your heart.

What about the music you listen to? You can learn a lot about a person by looking at their bank statement and his/her iPod. So take a look at your MP3 and inventory the intake of secular versus Christian music or Bible teaching going into your spirit. What we hear through music affects our soul for good or bad.

I recently read a poll done by one of the largest news agencies in the world. The title was "Sexy Music Lyrics Prompt Teens to Have Sex." The content of the article is pretty self-explanatory. Music with sexual lyrics led many teens to have premarital sex. Some of the more degrading music spoke of young women as if they were subservient to young men and that a young woman was to play out that perverted role through sex. Secular music will get into your spirit and cloud your thought life. I challenge you to take a prolonged fast of secular music. If you do that for six months, you will be very encouraged at the results.

I thought I was going to die when I chose to forsake Journey, Boston and Chicago. I won't even admit I listened to Hall and Oats. Did I just write that? Anyhow, when I made that all-or-nothing change in music intake God jumped right in and immediately led me to a brand new Christian station I never even knew existed. I thought the new station would only play some of the 80's gospel artists like Sandy Patti, the Gaithers and Amy Grant. I was obviously committed! But I shortly found out that God had been raising up some phenomenal artists, after God's heart, who were speaking to an upcoming generation of hungry believers. I still love and admire the older gospel artists and songs. Although I sincerely mean that, my parents would kill me if I said otherwise, and I don't want any mean letters from your parents, grandparents or pastors. The point is, within one week my near addiction to secular music was gone. I promise I'm not exaggerating. It was beyond a transformational and huge jump for me in my walk with God.

God is always bigger and smarter, and has unlimited resources to make the devil's offers as pathetic as they are compared to God's. When the music intake changes for the better, you will be happier, lighter and much of the goofiness going on in your hormonal brain concerning sex and relationships will exit. Not all of it, but a lot of it. You might think you're just a borderline pervert, but once again, you're probably not. You just have too many goofy things going into your brain through your eyes and ears, and it is coming out of your life.

If you put funk in, then funk will come out. If you put holy things and a boatload of gospel in your heart, then you'll have some blessed things going on in your brain and life. Make the jump! Steven Curtis Chapman's song titled 'Dive' declares, "Sink or swim I'm diving in!" Jump in and you'll be amazed to see what God has put in you.

Lastly, what people are you listening to and what advice are they giving you?

> *"Do not be misled: Bad company corrupts good character."* (1 Corinthians 15:33 - NIV)

Avoid the counsel of people who are more messed up than you are. That's like getting free throw advice from Shaquille O'Neil. Watch the intake of counsel in your relationships. When God wants to do great things in your life, He brings a person into your life. When the devil is on the hunt to destroy your life, he also brings a person into your life. Be on your guard. Some people don't want you to serve God fully.

I shared earlier about the perversion of David's oldest son Amnon. It is a fascinating and sobering piece of Bible history concerning the lie of lust, sexual perversion, generational strongholds and the influence of ungodly relationships.

Amnon had a cousin named Jonadab. He was King David's brother's son. The Bible says he was a very crafty man (2 Samuel 13). He concocted the entire sinister plan for Amnon to be alone with his half-sister Tamar so he could sexually force himself on her. Amnon raped his own sister. Disgusted with himself he then immediately kicks her out of his house, devastating her even more.

Absalom, full blooded brother of precious Tamar, heard about what happened to his sister. After two full years, Absalom's hatred for his half-brother grew as their father David did nothing by way of justice. Amnon's actions of incest were punishable by death but perhaps because Amnon was David's firstborn and because his own morality had faltered, the king did nothing. After two years Absalom killed his older brother Amnon for what he did to Tamar.

The demonic and sinister deception was that Jonadab was behind the whole thing! Remember, above all that you guard, be diligent to guard your heart from the influence of ungodly people. Jonadab was filled with evil. Amnon, cousin or not, should have kept a safe distance from his poisonous relative. Have discernment with who is around you, too. If they don't have what you want then don't be closely connected to them and certainly don't follow their advice.

In conclusion, 1 Peter 2:11 says to *"Abstain from fleshy lusts which war against the soul."* Do not invite any unnecessary battles to war against you! You have enough to deal with as it is. Deposit good stuff in you and you'll be encouraged by your clarity of thought and the good fruit coming out of your life. This will help you to rise higher in God, and therefore, will deal with much less pestering of the world, the flesh and the devil. Trust the principle.

Be where you're supposed to be: In the classic comedy movie *Uncle Buck* starring the late John Candy, he invites his border rebellious, and, for sure, angry niece to go bowling with him and her two siblings. His encouragement to get her to go was that it *"would be fun to get some fresh air and nearly impossible to get pregnant while doing it."*[1] Funny but there's some truth here. Just as Tia needed to be where she was supposed to be to stay out of trouble, we must be where we're supposed to be. We can get in a mess of trouble when we're out of our place.

> *"Like a bird that wanders from its nest, is a man who wanders from his place."* (Proverbs 27:8)

King David saw this failure played out in his life.

2 Samuel 11:1-2 says, "*It happened in the spring of the year, **at the time when kings go out to battle**, that David sent Joab and his servants with him, and all Israel...**But David remained at Jerusalem**. Then it happened one evening...*"

This passage clearly says that David was not where he was supposed to be and then something bad happened. He remained in Jerusalem when he should have been in an entirely different location, doing what he should have been doing as king, fighting a battle. Because of his misplacement, the Bible says in verse two, "*Then it happened...*" Know for sure that "**it**" happens when you're not where you should be.

David got up from an evening nap and walked along the roof of his mansion. He saw the beautiful woman, Bathsheba, bathing. As most humans are when they bathe or shower, Bathsheba was naked. She was intensely beautiful, clean and fresh, very naked but very married. Her husband was one of David's covenant mighty men, Uriah. That night David had sex with Bathsheba. She became pregnant. David tried to cover everything up with some maneuvering and when nothing worked David had Uriah killed. He marries Bathsheba. Some would say, "*Well, praise the Lord. His mercies endure forever. Aren't you glad God is merciful and forgiving? Let's move on and get over it.*" But unfortunately this series of sins caused David, his family and the people of Israel a lot of suffering. Read the passage and see for yourself.

What is striking, and most unfortunate, was how plainly avoidable these tragic events were. Sure, if all David thought about was women, then sooner or later he would have blown it. But David was a man after God's heart. He wouldn't have imagined he would do this to his long time comrade Uriah and his wife. David got out of his place and was not where he was supposed to be.

Listen, brother, if you're supposed to go bowling then go bowl. Don't be at home flicking the channels to see what's on TV at 11 o'clock at night. Sister, if you're supposed to be at home studying for your finals then be at home study-ing. If your parents tell you not to go to Florida with your friends for spring break, then be in your place of honor toward authority and don't go to Florida. Where is your place, environment, group of friends? What is your assignment? Where is your home? What is your job? Whatever your specific answer may be I strongly encourage you to be there and do it.

Please allow me to offer a little more advice. If some lukewarm Christian friends are all going this Saturday for an overnight stay at the beach just to hang out and 'have fun,' it's probably not where you need to be. More than likely some lukewarm Christian girls are going to show up with their smoking hot and non-lukewarm bikinis and you're going to get into some trouble. That is not the time to walk off together alone on the beach with someone of the opposite sex and pray together. It is very true the ancient proverb an older friend of mine shared with me years ago, "*The unmarried couple that prays together, lays together.*"

Where you need to be is home on Saturday evening so you can get some good rest because you got church Sunday morning! That's one of your places appointed by God.

Do not be critical of others: I will never forget a story I heard about in my late teen years. A mother and a daughter were strong church attend-ees. Unfortunately, they were both very judgmental toward young women who were sexually promiscuous. The mother was like the church lady on *Saturday Night Live*. Well, one day her daughter came home and told her mother she was pregnant. That night, they both committed suicide. I'm not sure if my youth leader just made up that story to scare us all or if he was for sure sharing a true story! Either way it worked.

The last thing any of us need to be is critical of people who are sexually ac-tive or who have failed morally. If so, we will be setting ourselves up for failure.

Galatians 6:1 instructs us, *"Brethren, if a man is overtaken in any trespass, you who are spiritual restore such a one in a spirit of gentleness, considering yourself lest you also be tempted."*

Don't allow your passion for holiness to pervert into legalism and back door you into sexual sin. Stay humble, merciful and forgiving while holy, passionate and focused.

Jesus said, *"Judge not, and you shall not be judged. Condemn not, and you shall not be condemned."* (Luke 6:37)

Be sincere: Many discuss the boundaries or lines of sexual sin. How far is too far? What fooling around can I get away with and it not be called sex? Can I commit every act of sexual foreplay except intercourse and still be considered a virgin? My friend this entire way of thinking is nothing but compromise and is filled with insincerity.

God deserves your best and too many Christians are looking to get away with as much as possible. Here's a clue, and something God prompted to my heart many years ago about this, *"You're not getting away with anything."* Be honest and sincere. Anything that intentionally stimulates sexual arousal is sin. Sincerity keeps us in the light. Admit it, quit it and forget it.

Honor your parents: Honor your father and mother. The Father etched it on the great Ten Commandments and Jesus affirmed it in the New Covenant. Watch what and how you say things to your parents. Love on them. Thank them. Pray for them. Look for ways to bless them. Don't judge them for not being perfect. Many good Christian parents faced devils you'll not have to face because they did it for you. You'll have your own battles to face.

All seven of us were unthankful brats toward our parents for a long time. As I hit my early twenties I began to realize that my dad, being a first generation Christian, was the spiritual pioneer for our family. He went up to the high places of alcoholism, which literally killed his parents. He went up to the high places of adultery and divorce that plagued my father's entire family on both of his parents' sides. I cannot tell you how thankful I am, to this day, I never, not once, had to face what my parents faced in their childhood. Thank God.

Concentrate on the good in your parents. Some of you had devastating circumstances surrounding your parents. I'm really sorry, as I'm sure it makes it extremely difficult to look for anything to honor. I can only ask for you to pray that God show you ways you can be that pioneer in your family. It won't be easy but God will make the difference and you'll have the joy of creating a legacy for your children after you.

> *"The father of godly children has cause for joy. What a pleasure to have children who are wise. So give your father and mother joy! May she who gave you birth be happy."* (Proverbs 23:24-25, NLT)

Give your parents a break and honor them. They deserve to be made happy by you. God, who commands young people to honor their parents, will also greatly bless them for doing so. Expect added protection too. Otherwise dishonor will lead to rebellion and sexual sin will probably find its way to you. Make it easy for yourself and value your parents.

Again, just like Biff Tannen, in *Back to the Future*, so kindly and lovingly encouraged his friend, George, while punching his head with his fist, *"Think McFly, think!"* I encourage you to think, too. Use your brain and decrease the odds of failure. It's your easiest battle.

SECOND: Friends & Environment

> *"Those who are planted in the house of the LORD shall flourish in the courts of our God. They shall be fresh and flourishing, to declare that the LORD is upright."* (Psalm 92:13-15)

Having God friends and being in a God environment are unspeakably great allies in your battle to resist sexual sin. Divine relationships and divine placements are huge heavenly weapons at your disposal. Just like a plant will flourish or wildlife will prosper in their appropriate environments, so you will be extremely blessed, happy and fulfilled being in God's chosen setting for your life. God has a group of friends that will bring the best out of you. God has a church, job, school or place for you to be connected. These things will bless you immensely and make you a blessing to others.

Pursue God for these things because not only are they a blessing but they are also for your protection. Godly friends in a godly environment help keep you preoccupied from idle time and unwanted opportunities for sexual sin to enter your life. Again, a battle avoided is a battle won.

Sports were a huge reason I didn't get into much trouble, including in the area of sexual immorality. I was preoccupied with basketball and baseball. The competition, games, relationships, passion for winning and hatred for losing were all a huge help and outlet for me personally through all my teen years. When I eventually hit my spiritual crossroads, God used the environment of my church and friends to help me get focused and serve Him with my whole heart.

Keep in mind God may challenge you in this area if your current friends and environment are holding you back. He might tell you it's time for a new transition. Be encouraged, though. It's only for your good. When God did this in my life, He immediately brought me a brand new group of friends. Within two weeks, it felt like I knew them my whole life. I was beyond happy and we had some great times together. We were also passionate about God and about living holy. It might not work out for you exactly this way; but God will certainly be faithful to you during this time.

You know what? We can get morally sloppy if we become idle, bored and unfulfilled. Guys can get overly focused on girls and vice versa when there's not much going on. However, God connected friendships and divinely planted environments keep you motivated and on course. Relationships and environments can be like a holy greenhouse of protection against unrighteousness. God is in the business of bringing people into your life that care about you, will pray with you and share your values. That sense of unity and agreement concerning holiness is powerful and exponentially increases your ability to stand against sin. You will be amazed at the integrity and desire for holiness that arises from within you when you're in the right place with the right people. God said that you will be a partaker of his holiness (Hebrews 12:10). You will most certainly identify with that truth when employing this principle. It feels great.

Some of you may think you have no real fighting chance at finding sexual integrity, but all you might need is a simple adjustment in this area. Go with the flow of the Spirit if God is leading you out from worldly places and relationships. You will grow by leaps and bounds and see amazing change as the real you comes alive. Again, godly friendships and a right environment will bless you, and are for your protection.

THIRD: Run Forrest Run!

"Run away from sexual sin!" (1 Corinthians 6:18, NLT)

When all else fails, run, dude! Don't accuse God of being complicated concerning resisting sexual sin. Sure, this instruction may not sound deep but it sure is effective. It may not make you feel like a strong individual, but run! Sexual temptation is not to be figured out or talked through. This much you know: you and that other person want to have sex together. That's all you need *to know.* Now, all you need *to do* is head for the hills. Do not over think this.

One time I was going to my fiancé's house. We were going to have lunch with her parents there after church. After I knocked on the front door and Kim answered, the whole world went in slow motion for the next minute, or so. In that split second, several noticeable things took place in my brain and hormones. First, I realized that her parents were not back from church, yet. Second, she wasn't expecting me to show up as early as I did and therefore wasn't wearing as many clothes as she normally would have. Third, she didn't say one word to me as she opened the door, but I was pretty sure she thought I was looking good that day. Fourth, the strongest sense of lust hit me in that moment such as never before. It was a set up. Talk about a "Sweet Jesus, help me!" moment.

As sure as I'm writing this over 17 years later, I only had another split second to act and run like *Forrest Gump*. As Christians we do not run like hell, since it's like a cuss word. We run like Forrest, instead. There was no time for "Hi." There was no time to talk about the pastor's message that day. There was no time to even try to fight this temptation. It was *run* or put a *bun* in her oven.

In one brief moment after the front door opened and I saw her, I didn't even break stride. I immediately turned without one word spoken and walked right back to my car. To this day, it was the longest, slow motion walk of my life. My skinny legs felt like two big redwood tree trunks you would find in the Sequoia National Forest in California. I can still see myself approaching my red Datsun '78 280 Z while that hot piece of juicy flesh was still at the door behind me. I remember thinking, "Don't look back Sammy! Go, go, go!" I knew then that as long as I kept walking I would be telling that story to others someday. Seriously, I honestly think that if I didn't run in that moment, our oldest daughter would have been born in 1996 instead of 2003! It is funny to talk about now, but it wasn't then. Your present battle is no different.

The intoxication of sexual desire is amazingly powerful. It should be. That's how God made it. But it is not your season to harvest your fruit my friend. Don't stand toe to toe with sexual temptation.

"All who were slain by her were strong men." (Proverbs 7:26)

Winning in this area has much more to do than simply being strong. It's like we said earlier, you will win by not playing the game. Run. The word 'resist' means to confront and oppose face to face. In this case, your godly stand is to run. Like Gandalph said, "This foe is beyond any of you. Run!" It may not seem warrior-like but it is biblical. Run and flee from sexual sin. It's how Joseph won his battle and how we will win ours.

Make Your Free Throws!

Ladies and gentlemen, please do the easy stuff. Don't get sloppy, careless or arrogant like Samson. He took for granted the Presence of God. He thought he could live like a compromising slob and still accomplish his mission while retaining his giftedness. All he had to do was keep his mouth quiet concerning the secret of his supernatural power. All Samson had to do was make his free throws. Sadly, he unnecessarily lost his strength through persistent sin. We can too. No *loosie goosie* for us. Do the natural and God will do the supernatural. Don't get overly spiritual here. Using your God given brain, the mind of Christ, is a must in this battle because, *"Wisdom is better than weapons of war"* (Ecclesiastes 9:18).

We need all of the focus and energy *for the battles we cannot avoid!* Let's go there now, and move on to part two but first let's pray and expect grace from our wonderful God.

PRAYER:

Heavenly Father, help me not to overcomplicate You or this battle for sexual integrity. Your Word says in Proverbs chapter 8 that wisdom is "plain to him who understands and right to those who find knowledge." I ask in faith and now receive Your pure and peaceable wisdom. Teach me to use it in very practical ways to obtain and guard my victory against sexual immorality. Forgive me for the times I have considered this battle impossible to overcome or saw myself as a grasshopper in its sight. I can do all things through Christ which strengthens me. I resist sexual sin in Jesus name!

Chapter 8

Resisting Sexual Sin – Part Two
Spiritual: Weapons & Armor

"Therefore put on God's complete armor, that you may be able to resist and stand your ground on the evil day [of danger], and, having done all [the crisis demands], to stand [firmly in your place]. Stand therefore [hold your ground], having tightened the belt of truth around your loins and having put on the breastplate of integrity and of moral rectitude and right standing with God, And having shod your feet in preparation [to face the enemy with the firm-footed stability, the promptness, and the readiness produced by the good news] of the Gospel of peace. Lift up over all the [covering] shield of saving faith, upon which you can quench all the flaming missiles of the wicked [one]. And take the helmet of salvation and the sword that the Spirit wields, which is the Word of God. Pray at all times (on every occasion, in every season) in the Spirit, with all [manner of] prayer and entreaty." (Ephesians 6:13-18, AMP)

For those of you who "sinned" (kidding!) and went to the theater to watch *Lord of the Rings: The Two Towers*, you might remember a great dialogue concerning the fear of facing battle. Aragorn, the future king of Gondor, Gandalph the White and Theoden king of Rohan are heatedly discussing the imminent danger of war against Rohan. As Aragorn and Gandalph are pressing the prideful and reluctant Theoden to meet the enemy head on, the dialogue proceeds with Theoden responding, "I know what you want of me. I will not bring further death to my people. I will not risk open war." Aragorn, battle hardened, passionate and totally right on says to the king, "Open war is upon you whether you would risk it or not!"[1]

How true this is for you and me. There are structures, embattlements and strategies already set up against you by the enemy for your destruction. Your battle is not in your future. It is presently at hand, whether you realize it or not. You will have to fight and God will give you on-the-job-training.

> "For You will light my lamp; The LORD my God will enlighten my darkness. For by You I can run against a troop, By my God I can leap over a wall. As for God, His way is perfect; The word of the LORD is proven; He is a shield to all who trust in Him. For who is God, except the LORD? And who is a rock, except our God? It is God who arms me with strength, And makes my way perfect. He makes my feet like the feet of deer, And sets me on my high places." (Psalm 18:28-34)

If your desire is to rise up and choose to live godly, then I promise right now that you will be challenged. You are going to have to go deeper in the things of God than you have before. The world, the flesh and the devil do not play fair. But then again, you have much more at your disposal, given you by God. There are more with you than against you. You have the Father, Son and Holy Ghost. You have angelic forces that far outclass the enemy in power, authority and number. You have the Blood of Jesus and the confession of your faith. You have the Body of Christ and the promises of God found in His Word. You have been given authority and power to overwhelmingly overcome.

Be confident in this truth that you have the advantage! You are in no way the underdog in this battle against sexual sin. Again, let's stop with the constant talk about how many young people are failing at sexual sin but rather see the Greater One indwelling you!

Our Enemies

For us to effectively employ our weapons and armor given us by God it would be helpful to identify our enemies. Granted, we were made in the image of God and are destined to be conformed into the image of Jesus Christ. Without question, knowing our Lord is our priority and primary purpose, which we will discuss near the end of this chapter. Yet, we are also instructed to not be ignorant of the schemes of the enemy.

The Art of War, written nearly two thousand years ago by Chinese general Sun Tzu, is considered one of the oldest and most successful books on military strategy in the world. In one of the more famous verses from the book, Tzu said:

> *"If you know your enemies and know yourself, you can win a hundred battles without a single loss. If you only know yourself, but not your opponent, you may win or may lose. If you know neither yourself nor your enemy, you will always endanger yourself."* [2]

For believers, our primary enemies in this battle against sexual sin are the world, the flesh and the devil.

The world: Primarily the world refers to our culture, the spirit of this world or age.

> 1 John 2:15-17 says, *"Do not love the world or the things in the world. If anyone loves the world, the love of the Father is not in him. For all that is in the world—the lust of the flesh, the lust of the eyes, and the pride of life—is not of the Father but is of the world. And the world is passing away, and the lust of it; but he who does the will of God abides forever."*

Again, here the world is not referring to the physical creation but to the sphere of evil operating in our world under the dominion of Satan. Galatians 1:4 and 1 John 5:19 together say *"This present evil age...lies under the sway of the wicked one.*" You would agree that there is a strong current of sensuality in the world in which we live. If we were idle in morality then we would soon be swept into the pull of the world the same way the current of a river would pull a victim in its direction. God did not create the world with its present darkness. Nevertheless, it is in fact dark, as are many of the people living in it.

> Isaiah 60:2 says, "*Behold, darkness shall cover the earth and deep darkness the people.*"

It is this environment and culture to which you were born. No sense complaining about it. It is, however, important to understand this fact and recognize it for what it is. We are not born into this world as victims or doomed to be subject to its darkness or standards. In verses 2 and 3 God continues the passage by saying over you and me, "*The Lord will arise over you, and His glory will be seen upon you. The Gentiles shall come to your light, and kings to the brightness of your rising.*" That's what we ought to be talking about! On the other hand, let's keep this in the center of our thinking: **the world itself does not afford you the luxury of living idle spiritually.**

The flesh: The flesh is also called the lower, carnal, or sin nature. It is our human nature without God. Your true identity is not your carnal man, but until you are given your heavenly body you will have a carnal nature to contend with. Your flesh has a mind and will of its own. In 1 Corinthians 3:3, Paul was rebuking some of the undisciplined and childish Christians by saying "*For you are still [unspiritual, having the nature] of the flesh [under the control of ordinary impulses].*" The flesh nature is controlling and attempts to force its will on immature Christians and unbelievers through its self-gratifying impulses.

An interesting story took place in the book of Numbers. A crooked prophet by the name of Balaam was hired to curse God's people Israel (Numbers chapters 22-25). Balaam soon discovered that he could not directly curse those whom God had already blessed! Instead he concocts a more sinister plan by essentially seducing Israel into cursing themselves through willful sin.

When the devil cannot defeat you directly, which is probably more often than you realize, he will attempt to pressure your flesh. If you yield to the dictates of the flesh, then he indirectly defeats you. Your carnal nature is not your friend.

> Romans 8:7 says, "...*the old sinful nature within us is against God. It never did obey God's laws and it never will*" (TLB).

It's clear. Our flesh wants to run the show and be its own god, just like in the days of Adam. Most would agree that, out of the three enemies, the flesh is our greatest challenge. Neither the world nor the devil can forcefully take your authority in Christ without your releasing it to them. Again, **our human nature also does not afford us the luxury of living idle spiritually.**

The devil: It is clear in Scripture that we have a present ongoing battle with the devil and demonic forces.

> Ephesians 6:12 says, "*For we do not wrestle against flesh and blood, but against principalities, against powers, against the rulers of the darkness of this age, against spiritual hosts of wickedness in the heavenly places.*"

To put it simply, the devil hates your guts and wants to steal, kill and destroy you. He is still enraged that, although he was once majestic in every way, he was cast down from that exalted position. Man, who was made in the image of God, took his place of bringing heavenly worship to God Almighty. God gave Adam relationship with Him and authority in the earth. Adam forfeited it to Satan. Jesus took it back from him and gave it to man once again. Satan is now attempting to keep us ignorant of that truth and therefore we have legitimate demonic conflict.

Undoubtedly, you've faced many pressures in life, but I can almost bet there have been times where you faced an adversity that was completely demonic. The enemy comes immediately to steal the word of the Kingdom from our hearts and we must contend to keep that from happening (Mark 4). Satan is real. Hell is real. While as believers we do not concentrate on him, we are also not to be ignorant of him, nor of his methods (2 Corinthians 2:11). We were primarily created for God's pleasure and worship. We would all much rather spend our time doing that than unnecessarily wasting it on the one destined for the lake of fire. Yet, let's not be in La-La Land concerning Satan.

We are told to be sober and vigilant because the adversary is on the offensive looking for an open door into your life (1 Peter 5:8). He doesn't come to spook you like Casper the ghost. He doesn't show up with a pitchfork and horns on his head introducing himself as the devil. He is constantly looking to hide beneath the shadows and work stealthily. His M.O. is smoke and mirrors.

Jesus describes Satan and his nature in John 8:44-45 saying:

> *"He was a murderer from the beginning, and **does not stand in the truth**, because there is no truth in him. When he speaks a **lie**, he speaks from his own resources, for he is a liar and the father of it."*

The Strong's Exhaustive Concordance describes the first bold phrase to mean that the devil seeks to "conceal and lie hidden."[3] The English language translates these original Greek words as to "*keep someone else unaware, ignorant and to escape notice.*" To lie means to "*utter an untruth or attempt to deceive by falsehood.*"[4] This how your enemy rolls.

In the days of Adam and Eve, Satan came in the form of something else so he could not be recognized. Today, he will seek to deceive by coming to you in the form of something or someone, too. This will require greater discernment and maturity in God to see through the falsehood. Thank God that Jesus completely and thoroughly defeated him.

> *"You were dead because of your sins and because your sinful nature was not yet cut away. Then God made you alive with Christ. He forgave all our sins. He canceled the record that contained the charges against us.*

He took it and destroyed it by nailing it to Christ's cross. In this way,
God disarmed the evil rulers and authorities. He shamed them publicly
by his victory over them on the cross of Christ." (Colossians 2:15,
NLT)

Now, we are destined by the Father to extend Christ's rule in the earth
(Ephesians 3:10). Just like I was demonically challenged with an unusual and
intense lust at Kim's doorstep, so you will be faced with a battle schemed from
the demonic realm. You can overcome, just like Jesus did.

A Winning Battle Perspective

First, as we step into battle, it's good we understand that we are not fighting
for victory but *from* victory. We are not contending to gain victory, as much
as we are contending from a position of victory. In a way, God, in Christ, has
already made you the conqueror but you still have the responsibility to walk out
that victory. It may seem a little strange but we are called to win a battle that
has already been won and your primary job is to not forfeit, give up or throw
in the towel. If you're losing in the fifth inning, God can always change that
scoreboard to look like His scoreboard, which shows us to be the winner. Your
enemy is after something you **already** have. Furthermore, he doesn't have anything you need.

This is important to know, as it changes your perspective and battle tactics. All at the same time, you are winning and have already won; protecting
the lead, and yet, are responsible also to increase it; and still see it all the way
through past the bottom of the ninth inning. God wants you to battle with the
confidence of heaven's perspective! You have the advantage because the Father
in Christ has *already* blessed you with every spiritual blessing, including winning
and resisting sexual sin. So you can be confident that He is maturing that eternal
work in your life, here and now. He is lining up your present actions, attitudes
and spiritual stature with that of your true and full identity in Christ.

This is not a play on words. See your battle, and victory, from heaven's perspective. This was the mindset that helped me not to ravish my future wife's body like a Meyer lemon with salt and chili powder (I wouldn't expect the non-Mexicans to understand). I came to the realization of a few things:

First, the devil was trying to get something from me (sexual integrity) and that there wasn't anything I needed to take from him (what I needed was already given to me in Christ).

Second, I already had authority over the world, the flesh and the devil and that no force could take that victory from me, except if I handed it over. This truth kept me from trying to run all over the place looking for the devil under rocks and turning me into a fearful and goofy Christian.

Third, since these things were true I realized much of what I was to do was to simply outlast the devil. My particular battle and victory was found in the resisting and not so much in gaining territory.

> *"Hold fast what you have, that no one may take your crown."*
> (Revelation 3:11)

The world, the flesh and the devil wanted what I had, but as long as I wanted to keep it, Jesus would make sure I would. If I didn't give my enemies my victory after the 15th round (in my case an 18 month marital engagement) then the Father will sound the bell on my wedding day and declare me the victor. You're fighting a winning battle! That winning perspective can serve as a tremendous strength in your specific fight. May God put this inside your spirit. You are not the grasshopper!

Now, on to our weapons:

Our Weapons
Let's Get Busy: Fight!

THE WORD OF GOD:

If you desire to win in your personal battle to resist sexual sin, the Word of God will be your primary weapon of warfare. It is your sword, lamp and light, your joy and wisdom, your healing and spiritual nourishment, the anchor of your soul and the seed of the Kingdom planted within you. The Scriptures are what the Father watches over to perform, what the Holy Spirit confirms, what the angels hearken to, what all creation was birthed by and is what caused you to be reborn. The Word of God is what will burn within you and create faith, give you good success, and make you wise for salvation.

The Spirit-breathed Word corrects and divides you, transforms and matures you, sanctifies and cleanses you. The Word of God trains the senses, defeats the devil and, by faith in It, we overcome the world (Hebrews 5:12-14, 1 John 2:14, 1 John 5:4-5). It is not to depart from our eyes, ears and mouth. It is to become more precious to us than gold and we are to treasure it more than our necessary food.

The great Warrior, King, Prophet and Psalmist, David called the Word: a lamp, a light, a shield, buckler, proven, eternal, perfect, sure, right, pure, clean, true and righteous; a comforter, peace giver in affliction; cleanser and sin preventer, reviver, strengthener, delighter, counselor and illuminator of the soul; heart enlarger; freedom, hope and life giver. Psalm 119 calls the Scriptures *"the teacher that makes me wiser than my enemies."* Jesus is the Word of God made flesh (John 1).

We get the picture: the Scriptures are your mighty weapon of warfare. The list goes on. We can, and should, praise the virtues of the Word of God, but what is our part so God's Word becomes effective in our lives? Remember, we do the natural. God will add the super.

Read the Word: No time to waste: you're going to have to spend consistent, daily time reading, memorizing and meditating on the Scriptures. Get on a daily Bible reading plan and stay in the New Testament for a while. Most Bible reading plans should have the reader on at least three chapters a day. Some of you guys jumped right into P90X after doing nothing but playing Xbox all day, so no excuses. Three chapters are nothing.

Do not be concerned if you sense no spiritual appetite for the Bible right now. Start where you are. Read the Word because it's right and do not—do not, do not—wait until you *feel spiritual enough* to read. Most of the time, it's the other way around. Just open your schedule and heart and begin a steady diet of reading and the Word itself will stimulate an inherent appetite for the Scriptures. The more time you spend in the Word, the more hungry you will become. Believe me, as dry as you may feel or as unattractive the Bible might seem to you now, God, through the Word, can easily change that.

> *"Your new life is not like your old life. Your old birth came from mortal sperm; your new birth comes from God's living Word. Just think: a life conceived by God himself!"* (1 Peter 1:23-24, MESSAGE)

You were conceived by the Word of God. It makes good sense that something in you is going to come alive by that same Eternal Word. Take the first bite, and your holy appetite will awaken and increase. We do the easy part by eating, while God does what appears to be the hard part by making us hungry, grow in Him and then some.

You see, by drawing close to God, the Holy Spirit will draw close to you, by making the Word of God desirable. If that isn't miraculous enough, the Holy Spirit will make the written Word become the Living Word in us. It will be written *"in their mind and on their hearts"* (Hebrews 8:10-11). The Bible will become living, real and personal.

Proverbs 1:23 says that the Spirit will make His words known to you. This is quite simply God personalizing Himself to us through His Word. Please keep this important truth in mind: the Holy Spirit is the One who gives revelation. Although we can, and must, cooperate with Him in this process through various Biblical principles, only the Holy Spirit is the Revealer of Truth from the Holy Scriptures.

> *"And all of us, as with unveiled face, [because we]* **continued** *to behold [in the Word of God] as in a mirror the glory of the Lord, are constantly being transfigured into His very own image in ever increasing splendor and from one degree of glory to another; [for this comes] from the Lord [Who is] the Spirit."* (2 Corinthians 3:18, AMP)

So as we continue to meditate in the Scriptures, it is the Holy Spirit who makes the Bible real to us and thereby changes us. The Holy Spirit and the Word are the Great Transformers!

> *"If ye* **continue** *in my word, then are ye my disciples indeed; and ye shall know the truth, and the truth shall make you free."* (John 8:31-32, KJV)

Jesus also said in John 8 that if we continued—not stopped for two months, but continued—in His Word, then fruit would be the result. There's a difference between truth and known Truth. If Truth by itself made people free, then everyone, including us, would be free, indeed! So what's the deal? Well, the Truth, or the Word, needs to be revealed, illuminated or made known to us personally by the Holy Spirit. When this happens then true freedom will explode into our world. Our part is to continue in His Word and pray for the Spirit of wisdom and revelation of that Word (Ephesians 1).

Now, take a deep breath and relieve yourself from any pressure or anxiety to force the Bible from your head to your heart. There may be times you're facing frustration in your devotions because you feel like an oil spot and God is the water and you can't seem to make the connection. Just try to relax. Be as sincere as possible and rest in God as best you can. Read in the Message Translation as Jesus describes the ability of His Word to create fruitfulness in one's heart in Mark chapter 4:

> *"Then Jesus said, "God's kingdom is like seed thrown on a field by a man who then goes to bed and forgets about it. The seed sprouts and grows—he has no idea how it happens. The earth does it all without his help: first a green stem of grass, then a bud, then the ripened grain. When the grain is fully formed, he reaps—harvest time!"*

Awesome. Plant the seed of His Word in your heart and rest in its faithfulness to produce great things in your life. Plant the seed and forget about it! If you took this passage and Joshua 1:8-9 literally to meditate in God's Word day and night, then you could wake up with exciting things happening in you much sooner than you imagined. You don't have to know how the process works for it to work. The farmer *"has no idea how it happens."* Do your part. The Word and Spirit will do theirs.

Read the Bible. Read the Bible. Read the Bible. Read the Bible. Read the Bible. Every day. Every day. Every day. Every day. When you wake up and when you go to bed. When you wake up and when you go to bed. When you wake up and when you go to bed.

Confess the Word: God's Word has some interesting things to say about you in Christ. Part of wielding the Sword of the Spirit is to declare God's Word out loud where you can hear yourself say it. Something very amazing about our faith is that, it was the very confession of our faith in Christ that confirmed our initial salvation (Romans 10:9-10).

I don't know about you, but I can't completely wrap my brain around that one. However, this inescapable truth resonates and is still applicable in our lives. The confession of our faith is somehow tied to establishing God's Word in our lives. Psalm 107:2 says, *"Let the redeemed of the Lord say so."* There are some promises from God's Word that the redeemed of the Lord are to "say so" out loud.

Philemon 6 says, *"The sharing of your faith may become effective by the acknowledgement of every good thing which is in you in Christ Jesus."*

We are to confess His Word, as to who we are, and that which is in us, through Christ. This is our true identity and our inheritance by the grace of God. You absolutely are who God says you are. We are told to share our faith aloud concerning these things. Hearing these Holy Spirit inspired declarations over you will stimulate faith and strengthen your conviction in the Word of God.

As this grows in you, there will be times when you are challenged by your enemies and the Word of God will come from your heart and shoot out of your mouth. Jesus faced and conquered the devil by saying *"It is written."* You will too. One good application of this principle is to read the Bible out loud in your devotion every now and then. Another would be to get a list of Scriptures that amplify who you are and what you have in Christ Jesus. After all, it is your true identity and you will see His salvation more and more confirmed in your life when you do this.

I remember one particular day when I was feeling pretty carnal, weak and sexually tempted back when I was engaged. I knew I better wake up spiritually or I might be headed for trouble later when Kim and I were going to go to dinner together. I began to speak God's Word in Romans chapter six out loud in my bedroom. I started getting into it. Then I remember declaring out loud, as if the Word of God was personalized to me, *"Sin shall not have dominion over me for I am not under the law but under grace!"* I declared it forcefully as if the Word of God was already true for me from that passage in Romans 6.

In that moment I found myself not asking God to help me or to make His Word true. Rather, I found myself speaking it out with boldness, in present tense as if what He said was not only settled in heaven for all of eternity, but also settled in the earth for Sam Beckworth! The Holy Spirit began to pray this way through me and I could sense His strength in me. It soundly affected my emotions and thought life. Something rose up in me and I knew that the Word of God was living and powerful. I knew the Holy Spirit was wielding His Word out of my mouth in that particular way. The lustful thoughts that were pushing me around that day went bye-bye. The real Sam-Beckworth-in-Christ came front and center. You see, God's Word is energetic, alive and full of power whether or not we ever tap into it. But God wants you to plug into its living virtue for yourself. Confessing that power filled Word is a tremendous catalyst to accomplish this.

Do the Word: Doing the Word has much to do with lining up your actions with your convictions. James 1:22 says to *"be doers of the word, and not hearers only."*

Follow your reading and confession with action. Thankfully, obeying the Bible does become easier as you read it and confess it more. When the Bible begins to come alive inside you, you will begin to notice a desire to do what it says. Philippians 2:13 speaks of this:

> *"It is God who is all the while effectually at work in you [energizing and creating in you the power and desire], both to will and to work for His good pleasure and satisfaction and delight."* (AMP)

What an awesome promise. You will soon encounter a tempting situation and sense His Word rise up in your heart and a conviction from that Word will strengthen your will and direct your decisions. When I approached my in-laws home and Kim answered that door, immediately came the words, "RUN!" My pheromones, testosterone, senses, and earthly passions were all trying to pressure me to push her into her house, lock the door behind us and get busy. My flesh wanted to yell "I'm so dang tired of waiting! No more!" But you see, a greater power, a prevailing influence, a supreme Glory was actively living and rising up in my spirit man. It was His eternal and living Word, His excellent Holy Spirit rising front and center. I was quickened again that I was the very righteousness of God Almighty and that girl was His royal princess worthy of royal honor from her future husband.

Done deal! RUN, FLEE and DO as the Word says. By the Word and the Spirit we put to death the deeds of the flesh. It was one of many royal crucifixions I had experienced during our 18 month engagement. Did that whole encounter happened in that split second? Sure it did, but the primary reason I ran in that moment was because I had already read it and confessed it 100 times from the Scriptures weeks and months before. So, my friends read it and confess it so you can do it. Don't get fancy. Don't be deceived. Read and keep reading. Confess and keep confessing. Do and keep doing.

Best-selling author Lisa Bevere wrote a very interesting statement in her book for young women *Kissed the Girls and Made Them Cry*. She said, *"We must know the truth with a greater intimacy than we've known the lie."*[5] Reading, confessing and doing the Word prepares the environment of our hearts for knowing the truth with enough intimacy to demolish lies we've believed about ourselves or God. Again, Jesus said in John 8 that you shall know the truth and the truth, that you personally know, will set you free.

I realize this is a ton of information. You might be feeling like there's already 100 things you're trying to improve in your relationship with God and here I am dumping on you another huge principle. In an effort to simplify this discipline, we've created a tool to accompany this book. It is a recording of many of the Scriptures in *Yes to Sex*. You'll find them to be in an encouraging and rhythmic order. In addition, the same CD contains a data file with the Scripture passages so you can either have them available on your tablet or print them out from your computer. This way you can personally read them aloud as well. Instead of trying to dig through the book and do this yourself, you can hear, read and speak the Word of God more easily. You can download it from iTunes, or find it at most Christian bookstores and at www.reachingforwardmedia.com. Let's move on.

PRAYER:

Prayer is a most potent offensive and defensive weapon against your enemies, including the battle against sexual temptation. It seems that prayer's highest priority is found in genuine communion and fellowship with God. We will get to that later in the chapter. For now let's look at how prayer is a tactical part of our weaponry and arsenal.

Overcomes the Flesh:

> *"Father, if You are willing, remove this cup from Me; yet not My will, but [always] Yours be done. And there appeared to Him an angel from heaven, strengthening Him in spirit. And being in an agony [of mind], He prayed [all the] more earnestly and intently, and His sweat became like great clots of blood dropping down upon the ground. And when He got up from prayer, He came to the disciples and found them sleeping from grief, And He said to them, Why do you sleep? Get up and pray that you may not enter [at all] into temptation."* (Luke 22:42-46, AMP)

Jesus said, in so many words, that if we would get up from our spiritual slumber, then we would not enter into temptation. We can safely interpret this passage in a couple of ways.

The first is that if we pray, we will receive strength to overcome in our present temptation so as to prevent us from failing. Although He was in tremendous agony of mind, Jesus became strengthened in spirit because He continued to pray earnestly. He went on to keep His will completely yielded to the Father and fulfill His assignment of the Cross. He passed the test! He resisted His will for the will of the Father. Jesus did not submit to His human nature as the first Adam did. We see that if we would rise from our insecurities and spiritual sleep in order to pray, then God would strengthen us as well. He will empower us to overcome.

Unfortunately we see the disciples sleeping when they should have been praying. Notice, however, that they were sleeping from grief or sorrow. It's as if emotional exhaustion was keeping them from praying at a very critical time. We wonder if Peter still would have cut off the servant's ear and then deny Christ had he prayed like Jesus told him to. We do know that he "entered into temptation" because he did not obey Jesus' command. Jesus prayed and passed His test. Peter didn't pray and did not pass his test.

When you are struggling in your mind you need to pray. Fervent prayer will drive out the sorrow or at least position you to receive strength for the temptation. Jesus said *"men ought always to pray, and not to faint"* (Luke 18:1, KJV). Praying will keep you from fainting and Paul said that we would reap our reward if we do not lose heart. In our weaknesses, the Holy Spirit will also help us as we pray. As we pray, we are simultaneously overcoming our flesh.

Secondly, it seems that prayer also enables us to avoid some tempting situations completely. When we pray, God can order our steps; our day and their circumstances so that we are supernaturally steered clear of potential pressure situations. Again, there will be plenty of tests we cannot avoid. Jesus could not avoid the Cross but was instead empowered for obedience as He prayed to the Father. When we become *prayer-less* we become *careless* and can run into a lot of unnecessary mess and thus enter into temptation.

However, it's possible that for every battle you face while leading a life of prayer, you may have avoided five battles and never even realized it. That's a good thing.

Also take note how the Jesus' fervent prayers released angelic help. Prayers release heavenly assistance.

Effective Against Worldly Circumstances:

"The earnest (heartfelt, continued) prayer of a righteous man makes tremendous power available [dynamic in its working]. Elijah was a human being with a nature such as we have [with feelings, affections, and a constitution like ours]; and he prayed earnestly for it not to rain, and no rain fell on the earth for three years and six months. [1 Kings 17:1.] And [then] he prayed again and the heavens supplied rain and the land produced its crops [as usual]." (James 5:16-18, AMP)

I doubt right now you are able to completely fathom the tremendous impact of your prayers. Sometimes we consider how weak or insignificant we feel and that our prayers make little or no difference. However, according to this passage, that can't be true. Admittedly, we all may have some learning to do on how to pray Biblically, but be certain that prayer has the potential to bring into your world explosive power and miraculous change. Don't feel disqualified for God's power due to your imperfections. Join the club. Actually, it is because of your weakness you are, in fact, qualified for the power of God. Jesus told Paul, *"My power shows itself most effective in your weakness."*

Circumstances in your life will change for the good as you continue to lead a life of heartfelt prayer. Beyond any doubt, there is a price to pay in prayer. Your flesh will want to sleep and your brain will want to check out, but you'll just have to dig deeper. Your destiny and sexual integrity are worth it.

Overpowering the Demonic:

> *"In those days I, Daniel, was mourning three full weeks. I ate no pleasant food, no meat or wine came into my mouth, nor did I anoint myself at all, till three whole weeks were fulfilled. Now on the twenty-fourth day of the first month, as I was by the side of the great river, that is, the Tigris, I lifted my eyes and looked, and behold, a certain man clothed in linen, whose waist was girded with gold of Uphaz! His body was like beryl, his face like the appearance of lightning, his eyes like torches of fire, his arms and feet like burnished bronze in color, and the sound of his words like the voice of a multitude. Then he said to me, "Do not fear, Daniel, for **from the first day that you set your heart to understand, and to humble yourself before your God, your words were heard; and I have come because of your words.** But the prince of the kingdom of Persia withstood me twenty-one days; and behold, Michael, one of the chief princes, came to help me, for I had been left alone there with the kings of Persia. Now I have come to make you understand what will happen to your people in the latter days, for the vision refers to many days yet to come." (Daniel 10:2-6, 12-14)*

In verse twelve, we see Daniel humbling himself before God, setting his heart to understand and praying. He did this consistently for three full weeks. From the very first day he prayed, God heard Daniel's words and sent an angel to minister to him concerning His will. Yet this angel was held up and hindered by a demonic force for 21 days. This conflict prevented the angel from speaking to Daniel and delivering an important message from God. However, as Daniel continued to pray, Michael, a warring archangel, was sent by God to handle the demonic principality. This allowed the messenger angel to be released and appear to Daniel and deliver the message and help him to understand it.

There is a war going on out there in the unseen supernatural realm. Employ your weapons of warfare by praying. Although Daniel's prayers were answered the very day he prayed, the answer did not reach him immediately. It took diligence and persistence in prayer on Daniel's behalf. Certainly if God wanted to He could have decimated that demon power and get the answer to Daniel day one, right? Of course! God is most certainly powerful enough. However, God has chosen to partner with His people in the earth to bring about His purposes. He has made us to be "*workers together with Him*" (2 Corinthians 6:1). Therefore pray and keep praying. Results will come. Our prayers release supernatural power to overwhelm the demonic powers that have been ranged against us. The devil will flee from you. Resist him and sexual temptation through prayer!

Pointers on Prayer:

There is absolutely no way all the great books in the world on effective Biblical prayer could exhaust the subject or teach us all there is to know. I won't even try to start. I would only encourage you to cultivate a consistent prayer life like you have been encouraged to do with Bible meditation.

Take a look at the Lord's Prayer as a model for prayer. Carve out some time every day. Although there is no magic formula to when or where you pray, let me offer some free advice. If you are willing, simply wake up a little earlier everyday than you normally would. Use that special time to read your Bible and pray. Even if you start out with fifteen minutes, I believe you will notice a difference in your heart and life. There is something awesome and unique about beginning your day with the Lord. It's like honoring Him with the first fruits of your money by giving God the Tithe. Try giving God the first fruits of your time by beginning your day with the Word and in prayer. No phone. No texting. No TV. No interruptions at all. Start with fifteen minutes and watch how your heart grows in desire and hunger. Soon enough, you will start waking up earlier just to be with the Lord. You will go from a need mindset to a love mindset.

FASTING:

Yes, fasting: no food for a specific period of time for the purpose of seeking God. You've got to want to win badly in this area if you're going to fast. Wimpy and sense-ruled Christians like to skip this *"unskippable"* discipline. Fasting is one of our weapons of warfare that drives the devil nuts. He can do nothing much about it, except offer you some bread crumbs and hope that you bite. Otherwise, effective fasting can destroy mental strongholds, drive out evil forces, clear up our brains, beat down and crucify the sin nature, clear out spiritual distractions and humble us so we can be more like Jesus. Fasting really separates the men from the boys and the Esther's from the Naomi's of the Bible. Whether it's for one meal, your favorite carb or a prolonged water-only fast, fasting brings breakthrough when just about nothing else can.

Preemptive Strike:

Living a fasted life is like throwing bombs in the camp of your enemy before he even gets in battle array. In his battle against Goliath, David *"hurried and ran toward the army to meet the Philistine"* (1 Samuel 17:28). David was not waiting for his enemy to bring the battle to him. David brought the battle to Goliath. This is what we do when we fast.

Fasting is a preemptive and proactive strike against our enemy, and an amazingly potent tactic in our spiritual warfare. It is an offensive weapon. Some of you may feel you're always on the defensive spiritually. As if you're mostly playing with a losing score. Fasting will change that. It will level the playing field and accelerate and propel you forward, instead of keeping you on your heels. Jesus said, *"I will build My church, and the gates of Hades shall not prevail against it"* (Matthew 18:18). Gates are a defensive measure of protection. As God's people we are on the offensive.

Through his sincere devotion to God, including fasting, Daniel shook things in the heavenly realm. There are demonic structures and strongholds set up against you and your future, including your sexual integrity and marrying the person God has especially for you. Your fasting will loose a heavenly arsenal to demolish those structures and make a clear path for you before you even get there.

A good friend of mine has been waiting for his future wife for many, many years. He has honored God in every way but wanted his woman! Within two weeks after completing a prolonged fast, God brought his wife to him and her husband to her. This dude was over 50 years old! She was a 32-year-old virgin seeking God for the right one too. Marrying the person God has for you is the second greatest miracle to transpire in a person's life. In this case, it came in a demonstrative way through fasting. Again, this is not about our works or earning anything but our call to exercise basic spiritual principles to see His will done in our lives.

Preventative Care and Proactive Humbling:

"I humbled my soul with fasting." (Psalm 69:10, ESV)

To humble means to lower one self. We talked about strongholds earlier in chapter five. Fasting lowers the high thoughts in our mind. There are irritating memories, noisy foolish chatter and flat out misguided reasoning that go on inside of our heads. We can get goofy in our thinking when we're resisting sexual temptation. Fasting is a proactive tool that humbles and pulls down that which is contrary to God's peaceable Word in our soul. Fasting is like taking a self-induced shot of humility and, boy, is it a relief.

103

Pride comes before a fall and I would rather make myself fall through fasting in secret than fall in front of everybody else through pride. Pride lifts you up and makes you an easier target for the flaming missiles of the wicked one. Fasting keeps you low and hidden in Christ. You also become more aware of, sensitive and drawn toward, the things of God than the things of the flesh. Imagine not wanting to please the flesh. Is there such a thing? Fasting makes and keeps us spiritually minded.

> Romans 8:6 says, "*Now the mind of the flesh [which is sense and reason without the Holy Spirit] is death...But the mind of the [Holy] Spirit is life and [soul] peace.*" (AMP)

There were weeks at a time in my 18 month engagement that I had no sexual desire for Kim. Among other things, fasting just took me to a different level spiritually and I became more aware of destiny than I was of my present desire. I also just fell more in love with God and it led to a stronger sense of my identity in Him, which is a huge sin deterrent. Of course, it was just as easy for me to get unfocused and sloppy all over again. Thankfully, consistent fasting is something we can intentionally do in advance to stay on our game. It is effective preventative care, for sure. Don't only fast for breakthrough. Live this way.

Presently Powerful:

> "*Then Jesus answered and said, 'O faithless and perverse generation, how long shall I be with you? How long shall I bear with you? Bring him here to Me.' And Jesus rebuked the demon, and it came out of him; and the child was cured from that very hour. Then the disciples came to Jesus privately and said, '***Why could we not cast it out?***' So Jesus said to them, '***Because of your unbelief***; for assuredly, I say to you, if you have faith as a mustard seed, you will say to this mountain, "Move from here to there," and it will move; and nothing will be impossible for you. However, ***this kind does not go out except by prayer and fasting.***'*" (Matthew 17:17-21)

What a great miracle Jesus performed on this child and what a revealing story it is for us. Jesus' disciples could not seem to cast out the demon from this tormented kid. But Jesus did. The Lord then opens up and says that *this kind* of demon, whether in rank or power, will not leave unless there is both prayer and fasting going on. Some demonic funk will not go anywhere unless we start praying and fasting. You already know that the devil doesn't play fair. I hear the nasty stuff some of you are going through. You're right, you can't just tell anybody, but God does want to show Himself strong on your behalf. He's given you fasting and prayer to help bring unfair treatment to your enemy.

Consider this: Why didn't Jesus go run off and pray and fast and then come back and cast out that demon? Because He had *already* been praying and *already* been fasting! The disciples were busy eating the twelve baskets of fish and bread fragments from the great miracles and then slept through their alarm in the morning. Not enough praying and fasting going on. What's the principle here? If we live a life of prayer and fasting, we will be more prepared to deal with negative situations that jump out at us in our everyday life. Interestingly, Jesus also makes it clear that their *unbelief* was also a major factor. There is a great case, then, that fasting and prayer also helps get some of that unbelief out of our lives, too.

These power twins provide power in your present. Don't even believe you're too young to fast. Your potential for greatness in your youth is a gift you can totally step into. What a rush! By the way, do not jump into a water-only fast unless your pastor, parents and other mentors are in agreement with you. I don't want you to get over zealous and hurt yourself physically.

Profusely Rewarding:

When we sow to the Spirit, we will reap life. God rewards fasting. Your fasting communicates to the Lord that He is more important to you than yourself or any dream you have. When someone gives up their food that's saying something!

Job 23:12 says, *"I have not departed from the commandment of His lips. I have treasured the words of His mouth more than my necessary food."*

When in secret you offer yourself to the Lord through fasting, He is blessed by your devotion. Although it is not your motivation, God will reward you where many will be able to see.

"But you, when you fast, anoint your head and wash your face, so that you do not appear to men to be fasting, but to your Father who is in the secret place; and your Father who sees in secret will reward you openly."
(Matthew 6:17-18)

Although you are not to put your trust or heart on riches, God richly gives us all things to enjoy. If you're going to serve God you're just going to have to learn to receive from His goodness. I have no doubt God blessed me with my wife sixteen years ago because of fasting. My wife is my crown. She is a constant testimony that proves I am blessed by God.

I still remember when my friends and some other acquaintances met my wife-to-be for the first time. My friend just graduated from UCLA and had about twenty friends at his home for a small, respectful graduation celebration. When I walked into his house with Kim, all of the talking stopped as they turned around to look at this beautiful young woman who was engaged to Sam. It was like a holy hush entered into that house as people, many of whom didn't know the Lord, recognized a blessing from God, given to me. After looking at her, they all looked at me as if to say, "If there is a God, we acknowledge that only He could have done this." Without a doubt God will reward you openly, too. Your promotion will be to His glory in the eyes of unbelievers.

Fasting, coupled with prayer, is the ultimate dynamo. Jesus went into the wilderness led by the Holy Spirit to fast and pray for forty days. He was confronted by Satan and the temptations began. Jesus finished the devil off and soundly defeated him at every turn. Jesus went *into* the wilderness *filled* with the Spirit. He then departed *from* the wilderness after the forty days *empowered* by the Spirit (Luke 4). Prayer and fasting together are explosive weapons to resist sexual temptation and empower you in the Holy Spirit.

VOCAL PRAISE:

> *"You are a chosen generation, a royal priesthood, a holy nation, His own special people, that you may proclaim the praises of Him who called you out of darkness into His marvelous light."* (1 Peter 2:9)

We were formed to declare God's praise (Isaiah 43:21). Praise is an exciting and fulfilling weapon of warfare. Praise is to be given out loud to God. If David himself danced half naked in public in whole hearted praise to God, then we can bet he also praised the Lord with shouts and declarations and song.

Okay, before you get too freaked out and way overly uncomfortable let's simplify this. You don't have to go around everywhere yelling, "Praise the Lord, hallelujah, God is great!" Besides, not many of us know how to praise like we should or at least think we should. The book of Psalms is filled with great praise passages. Take a month and read through the whole book. Many of the chapters are short. As you read, highlight the passages that offer praise to God. Don't highlight the passages that focus on man and how tough life is. That's for a different study. After you're done, try to include a couple of minutes of your personal devotional time reading out loud several of the highlighted praise passages as an offering of praise to God. Let's try this out. Read this aloud right now:

> *"Oh come, let us sing to the LORD! Let us shout joyfully to the Rock of our salvation. Let us come before His presence with thanksgiving; Let us shout joyfully to Him with psalms. For the LORD is the great God, And the great King above all gods. In His hand are the deep places of the earth; The heights of the hills are His also. The sea is His, for He made it; And His hands formed the dry land. Oh come, let us worship and bow down; Let us kneel before the LORD our Maker."* (Psalm 95:1-6)

Do it again and say it out louder and stronger. I'm serious. Okay, do it a third time but this time on your knees with uplifted hands. Don't concern yourself with trying to make something up or somehow think you should automatically be great at this. You are not being insincere or fake by reading these praise Psalms out loud. The book of Psalm was the hymnal of the early New Testament Church. It's as every bit as sincere as reading the rest of the Scriptures out loud. Practicing this part of our devotion will grow in us and praise will become a vital part of our lives.

Praise Makes You Feel Better:

> *"I will call upon the Lord, who is worthy to be praised; So shall I be saved from my enemies…The Lord lives! Blessed be my rock! Let the God of my salvation be exalted."* (Psalm 18:3, 46)

Praise puts the spotlight on God. This is what the Scriptures are referring to when it repeatedly encourages us to say, *"Let God be magnified."* You are more apt to yield to sexual temptation if you're depressed, feel bad about yourself, or have weird stuff going on in your mind. Many young men I've spoken to confess that they yield to masturbation and pornography only when they're angry or depressed. Thankfully, praising God out loud can help to flesh out these toxic and temporal emotions. You soul will be encouraged as you start to tap into the awesome life of God that praise brings.

The Hebrew word for praise is *halal*, which simply means to *praise with a loud voice*. The more primitive meaning is to *cause to shine*. As David said, our most basic reason for our praise to God is because *He is worthy to be praised!* As we do, we are throwing the spotlight of our attention and affection on God who deserves our praise. The more we do this, the more He causes us to shine. According to modern medicine, light has a therapeutic and healing value to a person struggling with depression. Praise will bring the light of God and the joy of the Lord to us as well. Read through praise Psalms out loud and you will notice a difference.

Praise Brings God's Presence:

*"But You are holy, enthroned in the **praises** of Israel. Our fathers trusted in You; They **trusted**, and You **delivered** them. They cried to You, and were delivered; They trusted in You, and were not ashamed."* (Psalm 22:3-5)

Sincere praise brings the presence of God. God is absolutely everywhere. Yet the Scriptures point to a distinct manifestation of His presence when His people praise Him. His presence will take residence in or inhabit our lives in a special way as we give Him the praise He deserves. Also, notice how the words praise, trusted and delivered are ordered in this passage. Trust and deliverance will follow vocal praise. It can lead to freedom from satanic harassments and bondage. Perhaps you've experienced this in a worship service. You sensed God's love and strength came in and then out went a lot of bad emotions. The presence of God will absolutely affect your emotions for good.

Praise Manifests the Kingdom of God:

What in the world does that mean? Again, Psalm 22:3 says of God, *"You are holy, enthroned in the praises of Israel."* When Jesus taught us how to pray, He said, *"Your Kingdom come, Your will be done on earth as it is in heaven."* While many Christians have a "rapture," *get-me-out-of-here* mentality, King Jesus has a *get-me-into-earth-and-into-your-life* mentality. The Father wants heaven to invade earth. The Father wants earth to look more like heaven. Praise is one of the ways this happens.

Praise is the heavenly *space invader*. Whatever space in our lives we welcome God into through praise, King Jesus will invade, along with His dominion, power and kingdom order. This is what the word "enthroned" is referring to. He is ready to manifest His Kingdom's order and power in the way most appropriate to anything in our lives that is out of order.

A constantly lust-crazed mind is a mind that is out of order, but His Kingdom can help make you un-crazy. Praise-filled worship is an entry point for His kingdom to come and His will to be done in our circumstances, thought life and spiritual environment. Listen to some great praise and worship songs from worshippers like Jesus Culture, Hillsong, Matt Redman, Chris Tomlin, David and Nicole Binion or Lakewood, and you'll find this to be true. Thankfully, there's a lot of great stuff out there.

No matter your religious or denominational background the Bible is very clear that we all were created for His praise and to vocally praise the Lord. The Holy Spirit will work with us and teach us a whole lot when we sincerely seek to be "praisers" and worshippers of God in spirit and in truth. He'll help you. Don't trip out with anxiety. Remember though: accept as literal the command to praise God out loud. No mumbling, murmuring, or whispering. *Shout to the Lord with a voice of triumph!*

Our Armor

"But put on the Lord Jesus Christ, and make no provision for the flesh, to fulfill its lusts." (Romans 13:14)

Out of this entire book I believe the rest of this chapter is the most important of all. Armor is obviously very important in battle, as it is defined as a protective covering for the body. Putting on our armor is part of our success in resisting sexual sin. Without God's armor any flaming missile of the enemy headed our way in the form of a carnal thought, sensual idea or any outright sinful confrontation would more than likely end up seducing us to sin. Therefore we are told to put on the whole armor of God that we may stand and win against the schemes of the world, the flesh and the devil.

So what is our armor? I believe the Scriptures teach us that God Himself is our armor. The **armor of God** could also be referred to as **God my armor**. David said of the Lord in Psalm 18, *"He is my rock, strength, shield, salvation,*

110

stronghold and support." Sounds like armor and a defensive covering, agree? David, the greatest warrior in all of Scripture made it plain: the Lord God Himself is our armor. He is our shield, protection and covering. We put on, or are clothed with, the Lord Jesus Christ, God the Son. I think being covered with Christ the King is all the armor we need. This is not meant to be a play on words or to dismiss or invalidate any of the great teachings on the armor of God. I'm just trying to de-complicate a very core and fundamental Bible principle: God is our defense.

So how do we dress in God our Armor? We clothe ourselves through relationship. It is through genuine and heartfelt fellowship with God that we put on our armor. Putting on the armor of God is not merely reciting an abstract prayer. You can quote a ton of Scripture and repeat a prayer over and over again and still be a sitting duck to sin and frustration. However, when we spend quality time with God and He fills our hearts with His love for us, then we become satisfied on the inside and covered on the outside. Our primary purpose for creation is relationship. A living relationship with the Lord is what gives God and man our greatest pleasure. Hearing His voice and experiencing His love as His child will warm our hearts and bring fulfillment beyond what we've believed to be true.

I was raised in church my whole life, but, at 16, I experienced God on a level I had not previously known. For the very first time I experienced personally the intense love God had for me. I was clean, fresh, new, light and could not explain completely how amazed and thankful I was. I never really had authentic joy in my life until that moment. I believed I was going to heaven before that but I had not experienced God in a relational encounter until that time.

Authentic relationship also prepares and equips us for our secondary purpose, which is authority and dominion. This is where warfare and armor comes into play. When we're filled on the inside *with Him,* we will be shielded on the outside *by Him.* You'll be walking with God alone in the garden enjoying yourself and next thing you know He's clothing you like Ironman!

How Does Communion with God Equate to Armor?

First: In a very practical way a satisfied heart is harder to tempt. It is also more difficult for the devil to broker a deal with a person whose heart is already filled. A broken heart is easier to seduce. The enemy's odds are better with an empty spirit. When we're dry we're much more vulnerable to sin. When full and happy, we're far more secure in our walk. Experiencing His Presence in a personal way will not only heal and fill you, but from an "armor" standpoint, you will not look for much else to heal or fill you. You already have what you need and desire.

When you are filled and refilled and ultimately find that He is Your source, you are less likely to look for the unhealthy affections of others or be deceived into bad relationships. As your relationship with Jesus grows and you more strongly sense His affirmation, you are less likely to look for the attention of a young man or sex with a girl to establish or define your value or get you to try to prove your manhood.

It is just harder to be disturbed, unsettled, agitated, upset and led astray when you're filled. A refreshed and strengthened young Christian can much more easily resist sexual temptation. A heart that is continually touched by God gets to chill in the crib of the secret place of His Presence. Psalm 91 says of that secret place, *"whose power no foe can withstand"* (verse 1, AMP). The schemes of the devil are more easily undone as they are found out in the Light of His Presence.

Furthermore:

> *"When a defiling evil spirit is expelled from someone, it drifts along through the desert looking for an oasis, some unsuspecting soul it can bedevil. When it doesn't find anyone, it says, 'I'll go back to my old haunt.' On return **it finds the person** spotlessly clean, but **vacant**. It then runs out and rounds up seven other spirits more evil than itself and they all move in, whooping it up. That person ends up far worse*

112

off than if he's never gotten cleaned up in the first place." (Matthew 12:43-45, MESSAGE)

There are Christians whose names are written in the Book of Life but their life has very little of Jesus. They may even be clean in their lifestyle but they are empty of a heartfelt relationship with God. If that's you, it doesn't have to be that way. Remember, a healthy relationship is one that gives off some life and excitement. It is ongoing, continual, daily, fresh and alive. God wants you to know the joy He takes in you and to enjoy your time with Him. Keep your house, the temple of the Holy Spirit filled up with Jesus. In so doing any demonic influence knocking at the door of your heart will have you and Jesus answering. He and his seven friends will be expelled faster from your presence than light driving out darkness.

Put the "No vacancy for the devil" sign up on the door of your heart. Walking in the garden alone with God everyday will keep a lot of them devils away. That's powerful defense right there! Relationship is how we clothe ourselves with God-Our-Armor.

Second: When God fills us with Himself, we are not only recipients but also vessels. When God causes us to personally experience His love, we then become a channel of that love. His love for us, received and embraced, awakens within us our love for Him. We love God because He first loved us. That night when God moved so strong in my life, I couldn't help but love God back. I never felt for God before what I felt for Him that evening. We receive love and then we manifest that love.

The virtue of grace is similar. Grace in the Strong's is defined as the "*divine influence upon the heart and its reflection in the life.*"[6] Grace first influences our hearts in a personal and intimate way but then continues on as an outward reflection. Therefore, when your heart has been touched by grace, your life will outwardly radiate that life changing grace.

Light, like love and grace, also has a reflective quality. Whatever vessel becomes lit also becomes a light. David said of the Lord, *"For You cause my lamp to be lighted and to shine"* (Psalm 18:28 - AMP). When we let His light illuminate our personal darkness, we also become a light and bring illumination to the environment around us.

These are just a few examples of the virtues of God that we experience when we fellowship with Him. They also serve to bring our attention to this principle: **We reflect what we behold**. We become what we experience. We give off what we receive. We radiate outwardly what has influenced us inwardly. There is a life changing experience happening **within us** through heartfelt connecting with God but there is a powerful dynamic transpiring **through us and from us**.

> *"But thanks be to God, who in Christ always leads us in triumph [as trophies of Christ's victory] and through us spreads and makes evident the fragrance of the knowledge of God everywhere."* (2 Corinthians 2:14, AMP)

We are manifesting Christ before God, man and demonic forces. We, as God's people, are radiating the knowledge of God wherever we go. Heaven, mankind and hell takes notice. The more time we spend allowing our Father to pour into us, the greater the intensity of His anointing we spread and diffuse. The more time we allow God who is Light to pour light into us, then the more light we will reflect and the more darkness will be driven out from around us. The enemy and his darkness may attempt to encroach upon the light, but Light Himself coming out of you overpowers the darkness. Light is armor. Light drives out darkness. Love drives out fear. There's no vote. It's as if light presses out the darkness from within and around you and keeps the yucky stuff at a distance.

I want to share a short story with you demonstrating this. Years ago I went through a personal and painful situation concerning rejection. It was a tough one. After nearly a year, I still couldn't seem to shake it. I'd have a good week and then it would blow up inside of me all over of again. I was a thoroughly defeated mess. The devil was playing pretty dirty on this one, too. Get this: I was quoting Scripture up to nearly 2 hours daily for about a year but I was still getting rocked. I fasted until my 6'2" frame weighed 130 pounds. I'm not kidding. We had registered nurses in our church freaking out! I was missing something in God and I knew it.

People will tell you to confess the word and don't receive the bad stuff. Well, I did that. People tell you to just use the name of Jesus and it will all go away. I did that. People tell you to speak to the mountain. I did that. People will tell you to just wait on the Lord, press in to Him, rest in Him, hold on, let go, release it to God, hold on to the promise, don't focus on the devil, take authority over the devil, go to a new church, be faithful where you are, sow a financial seed, pray in tongues… ay caramba!

I became perplexed beyond measure. I was not experiencing the peace of God and there was no way was my armor intact.

As I finally began to be brutally honest with the Lord about this He began to give me wisdom. Obviously, I wasn't listening very well. He began to show me that I forgot to allow my time with Him to be about relationship. I became so mechanical, formal and repetitive that I forsook the life giving, loving and refreshing qualities of genuine time with the Lord. I would spend almost two to four hours daily with God but was so sad and empty in my heart. My focus centered on warfare with the enemy and not enjoying the One who made me for relationship with Him. I was dry and empty and became susceptible to a bunch of pain. It was nasty.

I then became very depressed and began to veer toward a measure of hopelessness. I was not winning and it was beyond horrible. I tried everything I knew and did the best I could until the Lord graciously showed me what I was missing. What I needed was a relationship adjustment. I immediately sought to make any necessary corrections. First of all, I stopped making the devil my focus. My time with the Lord became about reading, praying, worshipping and praising,

YES TO SEX... JUST NOT YET!

being still and most importantly, learning to let God love on me more. The Lord began to fill me. It got to a point that even before I shut my cell phone off to spend quality time with God, I already began to sense His touch on my heart and His joy to spend time with me. My cup began to run over.

Check this out: it got to a place where I no longer felt the pain of that rejection, not even a trace of it. It felt like a dream... for three months. Because things began going so well I began to slowly back off my times with the Lord. It's the classic "book of Judges scenario". I went back to some old habits of studying only to prepare to give a Bible study instead of fellowshipping with God through His Word. I just got a little sloppy and I noticed that the precious intimacy was waning somewhat. Still, I was relieved I wasn't experiencing any torment.

Well, one night I was in bed just chilling before going to sleep and I sensed something in my heart. I prayed and asked the Lord what it was. I sensed His response was, "*The enemy is knocking at the door of your heart.*" At first I thought, "*No problem! He can't come in. The door is locked!*" That idea comforted me for the moment but what I believe God really wanted me to discern was found in my next thought: "*Okay, the door is locked but how did the enemy even get so close as to my door? He hasn't been that close in a long time.*"

This is where the Lord began to more fully show me how fellowship with Him is true armor. As I spent less quality time with God, the more opportunity darkness had to encroach on my soul life. The more quality time I spent with God, the more light would shine in me and reflect out from me. That light of fellowship, that light of armor was pressing back darkness that was causing me all kinds of pain. Darkness was where all of the yucky rejection lived.

Something important to understand is that it really doesn't matter so much what genuine revelation you receive from the Holy Spirit. If you do not walk in that truth and do your part to stay in the light of that revelation then you will lose whatever freedom you gained (Galatians 5:1). If I didn't get back on track and continue to stoke the fire of that daily relationship then darkness and all of the toxic pain would have overwhelmed me again. Needless to say I got back my focus and began to spend quality time with God! I did not want to mess with that ugly garbage again.

Keep the armor of light on! Keep genuine relationship with your Lord first place through the things we've talked about. It is without question your first and best defense. This is not a new doctrine. Please don't trip out. I'm simply trying to highlight a principle in Scripture through a personal experience. If you're not comfortable with the testimony then dump it and follow the principle.

So let me ask: what is your wattage in the spiritual realm? Are you a lantern or a floodlight? Are you flickering on the inside or shining brightly inside and out? Spend more time with Light and you will shine more brightly. It will make quite a difference in your battle to resist sexual sin.

> "*The night is nearly over; the day is almost here. So let us put aside the deeds of darkness and put on the armor of light.*" (Romans 13:12, NIV)

Let me add another thought: Being loved by God is the most important of all human experiences. Being heard, valued, understood and hearing His voice speaking to you will fill you like nothing else can or ever will. We cannot love God, ourselves or others until we are first loved by God. Obviously, God loved us before we loved Him, but God wants us to experience His love on an ongoing basis.

> "*May He grant you out of the rich treasury of His glory to be strengthened and reinforced with mighty power in the inner man by the [Holy] Spirit [Himself indwelling your innermost being and personality]. May Christ through your faith [actually] dwell (settle down, abide, make His permanent home) in your hearts! May you be rooted deep in love and founded securely on love, That you may have the power and be strong to apprehend and grasp with all the saints [God's devoted people, **the experience of that love**] what is the breadth and length and height*

*and depth [of it]; [That you may really come] to know [practically, through **experience for yourselves] the love of Christ**, which far surpasses mere knowledge [without experience]; that you may be filled [through all your being] unto all the fullness of God [may have the richest measure of the divine Presence, and become a body wholly filled and flooded with God Himself]!"* (Ephesians 3:16-19, AMP)

We will often need to be encouraged and loved on by God. It's fuel for us. Yes, we live by faith, by the Word of God and not by our feelings; but that doesn't change the heart of God for you to know Him by experience. Sometimes our *faith message* can get out of balance. I used to be afraid to tell God when I was struggling, for fear I wouldn't be making a positive faith confession. That's pathetic. Here we are in fear of being transparent with God in an attempt to stay in faith! Fear and faith are opposites! Some Christians who scream the loudest about faith are the guiltiest of fear. God help us.

When I was at my worst point as I faced that goliath of rejection, I remember being nearly incapable of speaking to God in a genuine and forthright way. Out of my mouth finally came these words, "How can I be transparent with You and in faith at the same time?" That's how backwards I became. His loving reply was, *"Your transparency with Me proves your faith and trust in Me. You are entrusting to Me Your very heart and life. That's real faith to Me."* His words to me began to unlock my muzzled voice and it marked the beginning of the beautiful relationship journey.

I know my Father loves me, values me, favors me and is the strength of my life. His communion with me is my weapon of warfare. The same way a child was created to be loved by their parents daily so we were made to be loved. If you are not good at loving others, if you have self-hatred or live in fear through insecurity or inferiority, then Love is your answer.

"There is no fear in love [dread does not exist], but full-grown (complete, perfect) love turns fear out of doors and expels every trace of terror! For fear brings with it the thought of punishment, and [so] he who is afraid

has not reached the full maturity of love [is not yet grown into love's complete perfection]." (1 John 4:18, AMP)

So just be at rest. God loves you right where you are. He is capable of causing you to personally know the love He has for you in increasing degrees. Don't be discouraged by not being perfect or if you get paralyzed with fear every now and then. That simply means you're still a work in progress and His love is still developing in you. Actually, you will be maturing in the love of God for the rest of your life. However, I do believe things will improve greatly for you in this area very soon. Ask the Lord to begin to teach you how to first receive His love for you. This is the most significant part of our daily bread. Ultimately, holiness is not the cure for sin. Intimacy with God is the cure. Holiness will be the fruit of that genuine intimacy. Remember though, this may mean you need to invest more time in your relationship with God but it will be worth it. God will help you to resist legalism and you will reap more of His life giving Spirit in a very practical, everyday way.

God is your armor, so get with Him today.

PRAYER:

Heavenly Father, thank you for giving me the tools to be successful against sexual temptation. You are always smarter and I give You credit for being perfect. I am so glad You have it all together. I want You to train me to be the warrior and child You have called me to be. Teach me to wield the weapons of warfare and to put on the armor of God effectively and consistently. I also desire to experience Your love for me in a fresh and new way. I'm tired of trying to earn Your approval and love. Deliver me from legalism. I want Your love for me to win over the fear that grips me. I want to hear Your voice of fellowship speaking to me. Reveal Yourself to me through Your Word. I want my relationship with You to arise to an entirely new level. Thank you for all You've done and for the sure promises of Your Word. I trust You. I speak words of life. I choose to resist sexual sin. I am more than a conqueror through Christ Jesus who loves me! Amen.

Chapter 9

To My Brother from Another Mother
What a Guy Wants

"Then Jacob said to Laban, 'Give me my wife. My time is completed, and I want to lie with her.'" (Genesis 29:21, NIV)

No time to waste. A young man wants sex. That's not all a brother wants but we do know the dude wants sex. Jacob was very clear to Laban: get someone to perform the ceremony so I can have sex with my new wife. He didn't say anything about decorating their new home. Jacob didn't schedule a meeting with their new insurance agent to get the new insurance policies. He wasn't waiting for a celebration or party. He simply wanted to make the marriage legal so he could go inside their tent, take her clothes off and have sex with Rachel.

Sex. More sex. Slow sex. Fast sex. Sexy sex. Sloppy sex. Sex in the moonlight. Sex in the light of day. Sex in the morning. Sex in the evening. Spontaneous sex. Planned sex. Sex before breakfast. Sex after second breakfast. Sex during afternoon tea. Sex. Sex. Sex.

Solomon said, *"Any way you want it. That's the way you need it. Any way you want it."* Come to think of it that was an old Journey song, but if you read the Song of Solomon, this young king of Israel made Steve Perry and the entire music industry sound like toddlers in sexual song writing. The point is, my brother from another mother, you're looking forward to some legal sex. *"This is from the Lord and it is His doing; it is marvelous in our eyes"* (Psalm 118:23, AMP). Sex is from

God and it is most certainly marvelous. However, I think most Christian young men would readily confess that sex is not all they want.

A Greater Need than Sex

Inside of a guy is a sense of destiny and greatness that goes deeper than the strong desire for sexual intimacy or even marriage. Solomon said that God "*has planted eternity in men's hearts and minds [a divinely implanted sense of a purpose... which nothing under the sun but God alone can satisfy]*" (Ecclesiastes 3:11, AMP). God created in you a powerful internal longing and sex cannot satisfy it. There is so much inside of a young man even he cannot fully identify with it or grasp it all.

There is a funny movie that came out in the early nineties called *City Slickers*. Famous actor Billy Crystal plays a 39 year old character by the name of Mitch Robbins. Although Mitch is happily married he's facing an intense midlife crisis. His friends, Phil and Ed, whose lives were in way worse shape than his, present Mitch with a joint present, a two-week Southwestern cattle drive for all three men. Again, three New Yorkers going on a cattle drive!

Well, after his wife insists he go, Mitch and friends travel to New Mexico, where they meet the ranch owner and several other participants of the cattle drive, including Curly. Curly is the seasoned and crusty trail boss. After a destructive stampede of the cattle, which was Mitch's fault, as punishment Curly chooses an intimidated Mitch to ride with him in the canyons to find some stray cows. They spend the night alone and surprisingly slowly begin to bond. Mitch discovers that despite Curly's tough exterior, he has a lot of wisdom. Curly advises him on how to face his problems: *by concentrating on the "one thing" that is most important in his life.*[1] Mitch takes his advice to heart.

The movie goes on and, after a number of crazy circumstances, out of the dozen or so individuals that started together on this cattle drive, only the three city slickers remain. *Instead of choosing to abandon the herd in order to preserve their own lives, they choose to face the unknown!* They crossed a very dangerous river, saved Norman the calf and saved Mitch who was saving Norman the calf. From there the three easily lead the herd back to the Colorado ranch. What a journey! They then went back to New York City with a tremendous sense of accomplishment and, for sure, an increased and healthier perspective on life. More importantly, at least for the sake of the movie, they had a new sense of fulfillment and a grasp on what that "one thing" was for them individually. *City Slickers* is a funny movie but also one with a decent message.

Many young men are in a crisis. Some are going to extreme measures in an attempt to "find" themselves while others are turning to self-destructive behavior to lose themselves. A lot of young adults don't know who they are, while others despise who they are. They are dying for something they can't seem to find and are searching for something they can't seem to put their finger on. Others don't know what they're looking for but they do know they need something and they do know they don't have it. Some are reaching for just about anything in a failed attempt to fill an empty part of them. Masturbation, pornography, drugs, sex, becoming enslaved to addictions and when none of it works they are taking their own lives or the lives of others. All for which Jesus died.

There is a heart's cry inside of young men that needs to be heard. This cry also needs to be clarified, understood and validated. We know that many are desperate but what is the clear and acute need and hunger? What is the "one thing?"

The Need for Value

I believe that hunger is for something called value. Value is an intrinsic need deposited within us by God Himself. He set value to be high on the list of our basic human needs and made value to be essential to our nature and constitution as a person. The Lord designed us all to be of value. This is definitely what I was after in my pre-marriage days and I believe this is something you're probably after, too, to some degree. We become broken without it but when this need for value is tapped we will sacrifice more than we can imagine to serve others or for a purpose greater than ourselves.

Value is a powerful need and it runs much deeper than our desire for sex. Perhaps it could be argued that you don't need sex, although you do need value. You desire sex. You need value. If you and God can partner together to break into this virtue, you'll not only grow as a Christian, but also be poised to stay steady through the various sexual temptations you'll encounter.

Valuing a young woman is a powerful deterrent against sinning against her sexually. Valuing her means you will protect her even from yourself. You will fight to defend her honor above your desire to take her into Jacob's tent before your seven years are up! It is much easier to value another person, like a young woman, when you have experienced and continue to experience your God given value. We'll get to more of this in a bit, but let's first further define this key virtue.

Defining Value

Value has a lot to do with approval, affirmation, significance, favorable esteem, good reputation, respect and honor. Every guy craves to hear that he has what it takes, he's got the goods and that he passed the test. Every young man wants to be believed in, commended and a hero. Value communicates this and says, "*You matter; you are noticed; you are needed; you make a positive difference; you are desired; you are wanted; you are chosen; you are well received; you are liked; you are an asset; you are a blessing; your life is a contribution; you can't be replaced; you are celebrated; you're the man.*" This is what people, especially young men, are after.

The Merriam Webster's 11th Collegiate Dictionary defines value in its most basic, fundamental and foundational verb form as *to estimate or assign worth: APPRAISE: to rate or scale in usefulness, importance or general worth: EVALUATE (esteem, to set a value)*[2]. This definition really opens things up. What I mean is that it's one thing to determine the value of a home, a company or an antique table, but it's a whole different world when the value of a person is at stake. It would be difficult for any of us not to become insecure if someone else is preparing to evaluate our usefulness or general worth as a human being!

Perhaps you dread getting your report card or doing an oral exam for fear of being graded poorly. This could be because you have a hard time separating your sense of self-worth from your G.P.A. Many adults fear work reviews, corrective conversations and even personality tests for similar reasons. We all fight fears of being told that we're worthless or useless. Although that's not what your report card or a work review is saying, it can still be tough to not feel like our personal value is being assessed.

As a result, many times we don't want to take the test or have it graded. We don't want to be rated, put on a scale, evaluated, appraised or go through a valuation because we are afraid to be told what we may or may not be worth! We're conditioned to fear any kind of conflict, even if it's healthy and necessary because we fearfully anticipate the words, "You *don't* have what it takes; we *don't* want you here; we *don't* need you; you *don't* measure up; you are *not* good enough; you are *not* celebrated, therefore you are *not* valued." Be encouraged, though, and please keep in mind that you are not your G.P.A, your weakness or blunder. Although we're to do our best in school or on the job, these things neither define your identity nor your true worth before God.

The point in sharing this is to recognize and acknowledge the desire to be valued. The key is the source from which we are getting our sense of self-worth. Who dishes it out and determines our value?

Who Assigns Value?

People *assign value.* People have a way of determining the worth of a person in their eyes. They have a process or criteria by which they evaluate another individual. Just as a property appraiser has factors by which the value of a property is determined (location, size of lot, square footage of home, comparable sales prices of other homes in the area, etc.), so do people, society and youth culture have their criteria by which they determine the value of a young person. Good or bad, and most of the time it's bad, that's just the way it is. If you forgot this fact, just go ask a young girl in the 8th grade about it. She'll tell you that her estimation in the eyes of others is weighed by how tall and thin she is, her body, her looks and the kind of car her parents drive or what they do for a career. For young guys it may be popularity, do you play sports, where you live, the clothes you wear or the size of your penis.

The evaluation system of society, and the scales by which people determine the value of another person, is quite interesting.

> *"The refining pot is for silver and furnace for gold, and a man is valued by what others say of him."* (Proverbs 27:21)

Imagine that: a person valued by the opinions of others! I remember in college a particular girl in my English class. She was very kind, well-mannered and to most guys, including myself at the time, somewhat attractive. College was flooded with attractive young women so she was just one of many and, therefore, nothing about her stood out in a glaring way. Her value in my immature and carnal mind was on par with the rest in regard to attractiveness. Anyhow, we all did projects together in that English class and then the summer came and that was that.

Well, one day during that summer I picked up the newspaper and there she was on the front page. She was the winner of the Miss California pageant! What?! I had absolutely no clue she was involved in that kind of stuff. Well, being the young man of character and integrity guess what happened? Her value in my mind and in the minds of many other young men like me on that campus and in California went way up! Her stock price and market evaluation on the college babe exchange went through the roof. Now remember, nothing changed about this girl. Her fairy god mother didn't help her nor did she get any surgery done to increase the amount of guys wanting to go out with her. The Miss California pageant, its influence and opinion, increased her worth in our eyes and her equity was worth her weight in gold.

How ridiculous, right? These are the scales of the world. The opinions of people somehow establish a person's value in the eyes of others. A person, common by the world's standards, suddenly increases in favorable standing with the mob and the masses through the praises of a few. They are unjust, faulty and imbalanced weights and measures; nonetheless, this is the way the world operates on a general scale.

> *"Dishonest scales are an abomination to the Lord, but a just weight is His delight."* (Proverbs 11:1)

God assigns true value. True worth comes from God. God ultimately determines the worth of a person. Significance and high esteem originate from God. Adam was not much until His Creator breathed into him His very own self. But once the Breath of all Life entered him, Adam became prized and esteemed high above all creation.

God has assigned true value to you. There is a bestowed glory on you that is not contingent on your performance. He infused His glory into your DNA and is therefore not calculated according to your good works. Our value is based on the Father's evaluation and not by our own way of measurement. God weighed us on the scale of His heart and determined our worth to exceed that of the blood of His Son. It pleased the Father to bruise His Son in order to buy us back (Isaiah 53). Besides that, God assigned our worth before the foundations of the world (Ephesians 1:3-14). This means our failures in life up until this point, our sin and rebellion has never once altered our value to God. He had already taken those things into consideration long before you were born.

Remember, brother, to be valued means that you are respected, praised and celebrated, not tolerated. God doesn't just value you like some mediocre nobody. *"I know you're pathetic and can't help yourself. I'm God and you're a loser but I have great compassion for you."* No way. Besides being untrue, that doesn't make me feel good. It makes me feel like I inconvenienced God and that He gave His Son for me because He had to, not because He wanted to. It makes me feel like I put God out; that I'm always causing Him problems or at least getting in His way; that I'm more of a bother and a nuisance to God rather than a blessing; that if it wasn't for me that God's life would be pretty good. Although these things are false, it is, however, a fact that many guys felt or feel this way.

We were born into sin and this creates a sin consciousness where we easily and unfortunately become more mindful of sin within our sin nature than His righteousness within our spirit man. This sin nature put us at an immediate deficit and we didn't even get to vote for it. We inherited it. So now most of our thoughts are bent toward what we're not, instead of who we are in Christ; how we're prone to sin, instead of how we're empowered to walk in the Spirit; what we're not good at, instead of what we can do in Christ Jesus; what we've been redeemed from by way of the cross (death, hell, sin), and not so much what we've been redeemed to (the Christ nature, seated in heavenly places, the blessing of Abraham, bringing the Kingdom of God into the earth). Again, since sin puts us at a deficit, our spiritual life can seem like we're facing an uphill climb and starting our race in God a full minute after the gun shot sounds.

But see, Adam was not the only one made in the image of God. You were made in the image of God, in the likeness of God, crowned with the glory of God, born again from the sperm of the Word of God, alive by the breath of the Spirit of God, purchased and made righteous by the very blood of God. You are not your flesh! You are not your past, failure, weakness, abuse, or what the world, flesh or the devil says you are. God has assigned your true worth, value and identity. Who you are in Jesus is far greater than who you were in Adam. God is right.

You choose who determines your value. Both society and God have ascribed to you a measure of value, however, only you will decide which system of value you will live by. You choose the scales. You select the appraisal. You choose the estimation. You have the right to choose the evaluation that says you're either a grasshopper or the one that says you're a giant killer.

Something interesting to consider is that God will often allow society and people to ultimately recognize true value He assigns to committed believers. The Scriptures say in several places that God's glory on His people will be revealed, seen or recognized by Gentiles and the world. The really awesome thing is that many will be drawn to the Lord by His honor on your life. Brother, this means that you'll not only be a champion in God's estimation but, eventually, also to those in the realm of influence God has specifically placed you in. This is not only Biblical but makes sense since God needs His people to be of value to a needy world.

Consider David. He was not always king. At one point he was even ignored by his own family. But when he was lightly esteemed he chose to embrace God's high, favorable esteem of him:

> "*Do not look at his appearance or at the height of his stature, because I have rejected him; for God sees not as man sees, for man looks at the outward appearance, but the Lord looks at the heart.*" (1 Samuel 16:7, NASB)

The Lord said this beautiful statement to the mighty prophet Samuel concerning the selection of Israel's next king among David's brothers. Here we see firsthand that God does not assign value as the world does. He uses a different measurement. God found young David's heart to be after His own. Because David stayed true to this, God promoted him so that eventually he not only received the esteem of his family, but his nation and the Gentile world.

God knows the language of the world and can speak it fluently. He loves to speak to people in their language. Some people in your world might still consider the Cross as foolishness, but your future employer can recognize the hand of favor on your life and open important doors for you. He might not know it is God's touch on your life releasing that favor but he will be drawn to you nonetheless.

Many times this is the doorway that can lead people to the One that has favored you. What I'm trying to say is, choosing God's valuation of your life doesn't mean you have to amount to nothing by the world's standards. God said that He would make His people the praise of the whole earth. Be encouraged and look at the lives and testimonies of Joseph, Moses, Esther and Daniel. They held how God felt about them above that of their present culture. God raised them up and the nations held them in extraordinary honor, respect and praise. Many came to fear the God of Abraham, Isaac and Jacob because of it.

I encourage you to embrace God's estimation of you over the world's. I'm telling you bro, your life has much more influence than you realize right now. God's glory on your life will supersede mediocrity and obscurity. Promotion doesn't come from the east or the west (Psalm 75:6). Promotion comes from the Lord and when He grants it, no one and nothing can ultimately suppress it.

People are looking for heroes. People are looking for others to do well. Even many in the world want good people and underdogs to succeed. People are desperate for life testimonies and examples they can cling to. They need to know there are good people out there. It gives them hope, warms their heart and gives them something to shoot for. God wants you to be that kind of blessing. I know you do, too.

A Greater Influence

A young man that feels validated by the Lord has, at his disposal, the powerful weapon of value to stay the temptation of sexual sin. The need for value can have a greater influence on a young man's conduct than his sex drive. I am of the persuasion that the guy has the ultimate responsibility to lead his future wife in the area of sexual integrity. It doesn't matter if a girl walks into your room naked and wants to have sex with you. It is your responsibility to run and avoid sexual sin. Listen, this is not only for your sake. You have her honor at stake. Your protecting her will cover her and add value to her. Your taking advantage of her through her vulnerability will take from her and deplete her of honor.

Don't blame the girl for having hormones, caring for you and feeling emotionally attached to you. Thank God for it. But don't pull an Adam-son-of-man excuse and blame her for your lack of restraint. God made you to lead.

130

You want the privilege to lead. Now lead when it counts and honor that girl! Everybody needs saving, including the girl you are or will be dating. Do your job. Thankfully, value is a greater influence than your sexual desires.

A Greater Satisfaction

Some of the obvious satisfactions of sex are pleasure and emotional intimacy. The satisfactions are pretty awesome. You might know them by the world's standards, but if you're not married, you don't know the pleasures of sex under God's divine order. But I believe value gives a greater satisfaction. Again, God's heart is that His esteem, bestowed upon you—your worth in His sight—would sustain and satisfy you above the opinions and estimations of others. And that you would honor and prize His thoughts of you above the approval of others.

John said that some of the authorities and leading nobles believed in Jesus but for fear of the Pharisees they did not confess Him, "*for they loved the approval and the praise and the glory that come from men [instead of and] more than the glory that comes from God [They valued their credit with men more than their credit with God]*" (John 12:43, AMP). God wants that to be at work in us, *except* the other way around.

This is the context to which I'm referring: When others may not prize you as they should, God's prizing you will hold you. When others are celebrated and you're not, God's delight over you will settle you. When a friend has met or is marrying "the right one" and you're still doing your best to patiently wait for your breakthrough, His honor of you will be enough. For the times you feel, or are, alone, His bestowed value sustains and satisfies.

Let's bring this into real life perspective now. I want to use John the Baptist as an example and a picture of a man who displayed this true value. He was challenged with great reasons why he could have felt he was no longer of use, importance or worth. John held onto the *one thing* so let's take a look at his life and circumstances as we find primarily in John 3:22-30. Before we get into his potential midlife crisis, let's look at this guy's resume.

John is an awesome man: He's bold. He's anointed. He calls the religious leaders of his day a brood of vipers. He rebukes Herod to his face. Most of all, he's hairy. He not only came in the spirit of Elijah but in the hair of Elijah! Jesus made a remarkable statement about John in Matthew 11:11, *"Truly I tell you, among those born of women there has not risen anyone greater than John the Baptist."* That is obscenely impressive. John wasn't a rebel or a coward that God just decided to touch to prove that He'll use anybody. That may have been the case with Peter or Gideon, but not with John.

He is not a wandering rogue: He can be found in the book of the prophet Isaiah chapter 40, some 700 years before his birth.

He is not unknown or obscure: He is the son of Zecharias, priest of the division of Abijah. His mother Elizabeth was of the daughters of Aaron with a lineage going back some 1400 years. Luke 1:6 says that *"they were both righteous before God, walking in all the commandments and ordinances of the Lord blameless."* John is their son. Most everyone knew who this kid was.

He is not uneducated: His father was as priest and a Levite and followed the commandments to teach his son the Law and the Prophets, as long as the age stricken Zechariah could. John would open up the scroll of Isaiah chapter 40 and see his own future calling, just as his father told him. He read of the ministry of the Messiah, the very One for which he was to prepare the way in Isaiah 61.

He is not a sloppy, carnal or godless man: He drank neither wine nor strong drink and He was filled with the Holy Spirit even from his mother's womb. He was dedicated as a Nazarite according to Numbers 6, Judges 13 and 1 Samuel 1. So we know that John wasn't riding a stolen Harley, cursing God, rolling up doobies and living in a van down by the river. He wasn't suckin' on some sea weed hanging out in a great fish because he was a rebellious or disobedient prophet. Luke 1:80 says that he was busy in his early days being passionately obedient, becoming strong in spirit, and in the deserts until the day of his manifestation to Israel! John's a stud.

He is not mediocre: There were signs and wonders surrounding his birth. His dad becomes filled with the Holy Spirit and prophesies his own son's future and purpose as God had revealed it to him. Even the people present said, *"What kind of child will this be?"*

Let's settle it. John is awesome. He's the real deal. Now, it is in this setting that John chapter 3 plays out. It's revival time and the excitement is at a fever pitch in Jerusalem. Most of this attention was centering around John. However, now we see the Messiah is made known to nearly all of Judea according to the Father's will and timing. John has borne witness to this passing of the torch and all of John's popularity is becoming the Messiah's popularity.

John's disciples run to him and complain in a near frantic tone concerning Christ, *"the one you baptized at the Jordan is now baptizing and all are coming to Him!"* One translation puts it, *"He's now competing with us!"* His own disciples are panicking because John's influence, popularity and ministry appear to be fading. John acknowledges that it is now time for the ministry of the Messiah to increase and his own to decrease.

John is potentially facing the biggest identity crisis of his life. For any man this would be tough. I don't know if John was balding, gaining weight or needed Botox, but we do know he no longer had the spotlight. His own disciples could have been submitting their applications to the Jesus Christ Evangelistic Association behind John's back. They needed job security.

A good question would be to ask ourselves how we would be tempted to respond under similar circumstances. How do you handle when other guys are more popular than you? What if all the girls seem to like your good friend and don't give you a second look? What happens when you graduate from high school or college and feel displaced or lost? How about when your best friend meets the girl God has for him and your mom still makes you give her butterfly kisses when you see her? When it seems like you're not *all that* how are you tempted to respond? Would you be depressed or unsure about who you are anymore? Every guy is going to face some similar pressure and times of uncertainty. John faced it but gives us a great example to follow.

Although we see John's ministry fading his sense of value, satisfaction and self-worth were not. We do not see John displaced, troubled or in denial of his circumstances. Instead, John reminds his disciples about what he shared with them in the past about the Christ and his role to prepare the way for Him. He exalts the Christ, talks about the Church and shows his genuine pleasure at all of it taking place. John says things like this through various paraphrases and translations of these verses in John 3, "...*I am filled with joy at His success...I rejoice greatly...this joy of mine is fulfilled...my cup is running over...*"

The big thing that stands out to me was that John did not get the girl. He was the best man at the wedding. He's an unmarried virgin with no prospects whatsoever and he's fulfilled beyond measure at what's taking place. Jesus is the Bridegroom and the Church is the Bride of Christ. John was neither, and seems to be more of an outsider but was pumped about it. He wasn't lying. He wasn't faking it. He wasn't rejoicing *by faith*. This prophet absolutely had some Holy Ghost momentum going on. He was on fire. This stud was on his game.

Of course we see that John's sense of fulfillment was rooted in a different influence. It wasn't based on notoriety, perceived popularity, the preeminence of ministry or a following. His value *from* the Father, his value *to* the Messiah and to the lost sheep of Israel was John's fuel. This passage is also very telling of two key ingredients that released true value for John that sustained and satisfied him.

NUMBER ONE – *Purpose:*

Purpose releases value. John had purpose given him by God. John knew who he was and who he was not. In John 1 and John 3 he says, "*I am not the Christ; I am not Elijah; I am not the Prophet; I am not the Bridegroom.*" However John went on to say, "*I AM His appointed; I AM the voice of one crying in the wilderness; I AM the friend of the bridegroom; I HAVE been sent.*"

There are a lot of things you're not, and it seems like we hear mostly about that side of things. But in God it isn't so much about who you're not, as much as it is who you are and who He made you to be. Besides that, who you're not pales in comparison to who you are. Our true identity and purpose are found in Christ. You have an exhaustless heritage when it comes to that. As part of your heritage you are also a unique expression of Christ in the earth with the privilege and calling to release that expression in your generation.

You're an original brother. Heaven sees you in a unique and powerful way. God has a picture of you on His desk and He wants you to see what He's seeing so you can become it. Heaven saw John as one with the spirit and ministry like Elijah the prophet. Please don't misunderstand this and show up at church and say that you're King David reincarnated. John wasn't Elijah but did come in that special calling, personality and passion. The Scriptures chose to say he came *in the spirit and power of Elijah*. Allow yourself to dream and ask the Lord how heaven sees you. I believe there's a part of your life, calling, identity and future to be found in some of the heroes in the Bible.

Purpose gives us a unique identity that sends us into His service. It makes us "value-added" and is deeply satisfying. Young men strongly desire to possess this. John did. He essentially said that he didn't need to be the groom to be God's man, nor did he need to be the main event to be rock solid. God can make you like that, too. Now you can be happy and steady when others are someone or something you're not!

NUMBER TWO – His Voice:

Hearing the voice of the Lord releases value. John experienced this consistently. John enjoyed hearing God's voice at an early age. When he was still in his mom's womb John heard the voice of Mary while Jesus was in her womb. John leaped for joy when Mary greeted John's mother. John heard the Lord's voice again in Luke 3:2 concerning the launching of his public ministry while in the wilderness. We see another instance in John 1:33 when the Father told John how to recognize Jesus by the manifestation of the Holy Spirit. Later in Matthew 3:17, John heard both the Son and the Father's voice. Who knows, since they were relatives, if John and Jesus spent time as kids talking about the Law and the Prophets and their respective prophetic callings. I just get this feeling John would hang on His every word as they'd hang out annually in Jerusalem. At least we know for sure that John loved hearing the Voice of the Son of God.

Hearing the Voice of the Bridegroom was a foundational basis for joy being fulfilled in John the Baptist. Hearing the voice of Jesus caused him to *rejoice greatly*. He said he didn't have to get the bride because he got to hear the Voice of the One for whom He was created. Nothing compared to it.

God wants you to hear His voice speaking to you. He not only wants to speak to you through His Word but also by His Holy Spirit to your spirit. He wants you to experience this dynamic part of your relationship with God. Just like His voice would walk in the garden for Adam and Eve, so He loves for you to enjoy the fellowship of His voice. This might sound feminine, my brother, but it is not. His voice will immediately release significance into you. The Lord's voice locates you and causes you to be found. It releases joy. You experience His love and sense of affirmation in a dramatic and new way.

The first time I heard the Lord's voice I was going through a year-long fiery trial concerning guilt, condemnation and shame about twenty years ago. As I prayed and studied the Scriptures diligently for months He said to my heart, "To many people, sin and the temptation to sin are one in the same." You see I was already feeling like I sinned against God as soon as I began to experience feelings of guilt, shame and condemnation. I would just immediately give in to misery without a fight, wondering once again what I was doing wrong and why was I such a disappointment to God!

When I heard His voice for the first time as He spoke those words I was so overwhelmed that my focus wasn't even so much on the specific instruction as it was on all the love and life that came with His words. His words brought freedom to me. I realized I hadn't sinned against the Lord for simply being confronted by the toxic emotions! More significantly was the initial lesson that God wants me to fellowship in His Word and also for Him to fellowship with me by speaking to me.

> "*Your words were found, and I ate them, and Your word to me was the joy and rejoicing of my heart.*" (Jeremiah 15:16)

His voice may not be primarily for instruction as much as for fellowship. John heard the Lord's voice tell him about His public ministry to Israel. No doubt it was an exhilarating experience! Obviously, it was. He preached with intense boldness knowing He heard from God and He was going to fulfill the will of God in His life! But His voice that brought joy to John as a baby in the womb, His voice that gave John companionship in the wilderness after no doubt his very old parents had passed away, His voice that brought great rejoicing to John as a best man for a best friend marrying His bride, is no doubt the Voice of fellowship and communion. Your primary destiny is an intimate relationship with God. It's then time to extend the Kingdom through our calling and purpose discovered by that relationship.

Hearing the Lord's Voice gives value to a young man that satisfies. It is what makes us feel valued by God. Purpose and the fellowship of God's voice satisfied and sustained John. It kept him on course and it can keep you on course, too.

A Greater Pleasure

> "*A man can receive nothing [he can claim nothing, he can take unto himself nothing] except as it has been granted to him from heaven. [A man must be content to receive **the gift which is given** him **from heaven**; there is no other source.]...This then **is my pleasure** and my joy.*" (John 3:27, 29, AMP)

John's life pleasure was found in what God gave him. Heaven allotted John a special fellowship with God and a special calling. John's fulfillment was in that which heaven gave him. I'm sure it wasn't all perfect. He had very old parents, who probably died when he was still young. He lived in the Judean wilderness and not in Jerusalem or in Galilee. His steady diet was locusts and not Chick-fil-a. He had a powerful prophetic ministry but it was very confrontational and it came with a price. Nevertheless, John tapped into the greater pleasure. He was content to receive the gift given him and his pleasure and joy over his part was in overflow mode.

You do not want what heaven hasn't given you. You do not want a girl that God hasn't willed for you. Your greater pleasure is found in what God has given you, not in what God hasn't given you. You don't want to be what heaven has not made you to be. So be watchful not to covet what your buddy in your small group has, and to not be resentful over what you don't have. It might seem like everybody else has it all together and you might feel like you're all over the place. Don't sweat it, brother. God is making you what you ought to be and He's pleased with you even in the middle of the process. Press into Him through your weapons of warfare and His voice will come to you like it did for John.

God designed your destiny as such that your fulfillment, your happiness and joy are resident within what God gives. A specific grace, special fellowship and purpose are wrapped up in a present that heaven has gifted especially for you. You cannot be happy trying to be someone else. This is a huge deal so don't get overly frustrated if it takes a while for you to step into your DNA in God. If it were easy everybody would be true to who God made them to be but many guys don't know who they are yet or are not comfortable in their own skin. It's like going through spiritual puberty. This is why many are trying to find it through other means, like sex outside of God's original intent. Others are trying to force the issue and date or seek to marry someone heaven hasn't given them. This can create a colossal mess and take years to recover from.

It's true that you might not be ready yet for your wife, but believe me; she might not be ready for you, either. She might still need some maturing herself. In the book, *The Right Guy for the Right Girl*, authors Jackie Kendall and Debby Jones said it well, "*Men, God has made you princes in His Kingdom. Your job is not to go searching for a damsel in distress. In fact a damsel constantly in distress might be a warning sign that her focus and maturity are not where they need to be."*[2]

Many men, young and old, look for their validation from a female. They have a savior complex. They feel like a real man when a girl really needs him. He feels extra spiritual if the girl is broken since now he can minister to her. She thinks he's the International Christian of the Year. However, your first ministry is to God. Your deepest sense of validation comes from God not from any other person. A young woman, if we first receive our glory and praise from God, will testify and bear witness of that validation, but your sense of honor won't originate from her. God's honor on your life will satisfy you well beyond what a girl can. When a young man's life is ordered this way, when the time comes for a young woman to be brought into your life, it will truly be awesome!

A Greater Source

"...*God alone can satisfy...*" (Ecclesiastes 3:11, AMP)

Young men driven by sex are not experiencing their value because sex does not validate your worth. It does not make you a real man. But when we are first valued by God, then our sexual conduct and desires can be ordered Biblically. The ongoing and experiential knowledge of God's approval on your life will help you to eventually enjoy sex, yet not be controlled by it. God created sex to be pleasurable not a domineering lust.

The worth that God assigns is a greater source than the testimony of people. Only God can satisfy what He put in you. For sure it will take some major focus to consistently tap into this but you can do it. You need to do this because sex seems so intricately tied to manhood and personal validation that it can be difficult to separate the two.

On a more mild level, it's just nice and encouraging when a girl even expresses interest in you. Isn't it true? It's powerful. She's speaking value to you as she says, "I think you're worth a lot." Sincere and complimentary attractions like that can have an astounding pull on your heart. This is why I chose to be dateless for years. I thought I would turn into Jell-O if a girl looked me in the eye, took my hand and told me sincerely I was handsome. I knew if I had any wiggle room to date it would have been over for me. I had a lot of growing up to do to even handle a nice compliment. I'm sure you're better at it than I was.

Of course on a more serious level, from my teenage years until the time I was married, I had to battle, though at varying levels of intensity, the thought that, if I was a real man, I would become sexually active. No wonder we need to allow the Lord to consistently communicate to us our worth to Him. My brother from another mother, you're God's man! Just accept it and let it be settled in your heart.

PRAYER:

"Heavenly Father, I desire to experience Your validation. I am hungry to hear Your voice. I am passionate about seeing myself as heaven does. My expectation is in You. You are my source for esteem and worth. Grace me to receive all that You have for me and all that You've made me to be. Help me to know by experience and on a personal level Your approval of me. May I hear Your words, 'Well, done my son. In you I am well pleased.' In this, I ask for You to heal any father wounds I may have. Lead me into freedom from all shame, guilt and condemnation. I want You to fill every part of my life. I want to fulfill Your will in my generation. In Jesus name, Amen."

Chapter 10

To My Sister from Another Mister
A Special Message for the Girls

I am so glad to be sharing a special word with you. You're my sister in Christ and my prayer is that you would genuinely experience God's best for your life. I really do feel like your ally. That probably sounds weird but I've heard about a lot of junk you're facing, including the epidemic of the scarcity of good guys out there. Considering the times we live in, I'm pretty sure you could use some encouraging words, especially concerning a special young man in your future.

You have so much to offer your generation. Although you may have a harder time seeing it right now, you also have a lot to offer your future husband. Some young man is already trusting God that one day you'll be in his life. You are being sought out and prayed for by *the right one*. Hopefully God will use this chapter as inspiration for you.

You are Special

You are uniquely special. This was God's doing. He made you this way. As you recognize this and see yourself more clearly through His eyes you are less likely to look for a young man to establish your value or worth.

In my opinion it seems like girls live in a rough world. I do not nor have I ever envied it. Your environments can get flat out nasty. In her National Bestseller

Odd Girl Out: The Hidden Culture of Aggression in Girls, Rachel Simmons had some painfully raw and revealing facts to share concerning the world of teen girls:

> *"There is a hidden culture of girls' aggression in which bullying is epidemic, distinctive, and destructive. It is not marked by the direct verbal and physical behavior that is primarily the province of boys. Our culture refuses girls access to open conflict, and it forces their aggression into nonphysical, indirect, and covert forms. Girls use backbiting, exclusion, rumors, name-calling, and manipulation to inflict psychological pain on victimized targets. Unlike boys, who tend to bully acquaintances or strangers, girls frequently attack within tightly knit networks of friends, making aggression harder to identify and intensifying the damage to the targets. Within the culture of aggression, girls fight with body language and relationships instead of fists and knives. In this world, friendship is a weapon, and the sting of a shout pales in comparison to a day of someone's silence. There is no gesture more devastating than the back turning away."[1]*

I'm glad I'm a guy. Yeah, some guys are jerks but some girls just don't play fair. Girls can be mean in a dark way. Many are insecure and hide behind their looks. Yet even the more popular girls can find it nearly impossible to find a genuine, trustworthy and caring friend. Unfortunately, if you can't find good friends then you may turn to boys in relationships. If you have felt repeatedly rejected by girls then you may look for guys to fill that void of loneliness. Sexual activity is likely to follow. He wants your body and, although sexual sin may be pleasurable to you as well, you are probably looking to fill a deeper need like being loved, liked or accepted. Your connection is emotionally driven and so many Christian young women will compromise in this way even though the affection received is a cheap imitation for the real deal. Unfortunately, in these situations a girl is more likely to be used and less likely to be loved. I want you to know that God hurts with you and feels the pain you are now facing. He cares so much for you.

CHAPTER 10

Thankfully, God is the one who establishes value in people. I pray you would believe that you do not need to give your body to a young man because God is more than able and willing to fill that part of your heart. God will bring you good friends. He will bring you a godly husband. You were made to have these relationships. But you also have within you a "God love-tank" that only He can fill. Only God can give you a deep sense of validation, acceptance and self-worth. Sure, the fact that a guy may find you attractive can, and should, be flattering but it will never touch that part of you God made for Himself.

In her book *Your Knight in Shining Armor*, P.B. Wilson wrote:

> *"We long for someone who loves us, understands us, listens to us, provides for us, protects us, cares for us - is crazy about us! God gives these desires. Don't you think the One who instills the desires knows how to fulfill them?"*[2]

God will give you the sense of security, wholeness and companionship that ultimately comes from Him. This companionship with God can also help maintain or regain your sexual integrity.

> *"He brought me to the banqueting house, and his banner over me was love [for love waved as a protecting and comforting banner over my head when I was near him]."* (Song of Solomon 2:4, AMP)

So stay near to Him. His love will be protection and comfort to you. His love will cause you to believe that you're special, because He said so.

You are Desired

You are especially attractive. God made you desirable. God designed you to be beautiful and so young men are going to be attracted to you. You are not a sex object, but as a young woman, God made you desirable. 1 Corinthians 11:7 says that *"man's glory is the woman"* (TLB). This, in part, means that a woman,

Among many things, will complement her eventual husband. He will look better, be better thought of and more highly esteemed by others because you will one day be in his life. The worth of your future husband will drastically increase because of you. One Greek dictionary defines glory as *an appearance commanding respect, magnificence and excellence.* These are the qualities God, your Creator, already graced you with.

> *"I am my beloved's and **his desire is toward me.**"* (Song of Solomon 7:10)

Young men are going to be sexually attracted to you. This desire does not make him an undisciplined Christian. God made you with plenty of curves. Respectfully, your body alone is enough to force even the best of young men to take a deep breath to maintain his composure. I'm pretty sure you don't mind that too much since young women want to feel pretty and considered attractive.

There are quite a few stories in the Bible of attractive women. Sarai was close to ninety years old when she looked like she just walked out of the Cosmopolitan office with a new twenty year contract. The Bible says of Rebekah and Rachel that they were *very beautiful to behold in form and appearance.* The name Rebekah means 'captivating' and so she was. Jacob was so overwhelmed by Rachel's beauty that he worked for her father for seven years in order to marry her. To Jacob seven years *"seemed only a few days to him because of the love he had for her"* (Genesis 29:20-21).

Wow. Now, don't hate these girls because they were beautiful. God made them that way. As a matter of truth, young women who are considered attractive can have even more difficulties to deal with. If that's you, you might be constantly challenged with pressure from young men to date, horrible jealousy from peers, being misunderstood or mischaracterized, resulting in an unfair measure of loneliness. It's almost like being dealt persecution for God making you beautiful according to the world's standards. Just because it may not be difficult for you to get a guy's attention doesn't mean that you don't cry yourself to sleep at night for a lack of genuine friendships. You also need and have God's special attention, too.

Now, what about the girls who *don't* get all the attention from guys or the popular crowd? The big question, and one that warrants an answer, is what happens if you don't feel pretty or may not be pretty according to the standards of a young woman's model magazine? Well, thankfully just as God establishes your value and makes you special, God's favor on your life can also make you attractive.

In Scripture we find this girl named Leah. She is Rachel's older sister. What we see first about Leah is that she is not attractive in appearance like her sister. Secondly, after they both become Jacob's wives Leah was not loved by Jacob like her sister Rachel. Verse 31 actually says that Leah was unloved. To make matters worse the name Leah in the Hebrew language means *"to weary, to tire or make disgusted."*[3] Ouch. She was definitely facing an uphill climb. How many young women find themselves feeling like Leah? Many, I'm sure. So, how can God intervene if one feels unattractive and lightly esteemed? Does God even care? Sure, He does!

In Leah's case God saw that she was unloved and so brought life through her. For some reason both sisters were barren. God, the Giver of Life, opened her womb and blessed her to have many children with Jacob. Bearing children was a sign of great honor, blessing and favor in that culture. Leah was convincingly honored by God and God used this honor to somehow cause Jacob to not only love, but also be attracted to his wife. Jacob was obviously insensitive, hurtful and selfish for his early attitude toward Leah but let's try not to focus on that right now. Rather, let's concentrate on the progression of Leah's increased attraction in his eyes by God's hand on her life.

Leah's first son, Reuben, is born. His name means, "See, a son." She said that God **looked** on her affliction and saw the pain of being unloved and outwardly unattractive compared to her sister. It's as if she's holding their son as she presents Reuben to Jacob saying, *"See, a son. Will you please love me now? Look,*

I've given you your firstborn son. Please love me." God knows you want to be loved by someone special in your future, too.

Next she gives birth to Simeon, which means "heard." She said God **heard** that she was still unloved and blessed her again with another son. She begins to know firsthand that God sees, hears and takes to heart her rejection and hurtful circumstances. Although it appears that Jacob hasn't changed much yet, Leah's personal experiences with God, throughout her challenges and childbearing has proven an encouragement as noted by the names of her sons.

God also knows your pain and insecurities and He cares very much. Allowing God to meet you in hurtful circumstances will be a great encouragement to you, too. Just as Leah allowed God to see and hear her in her difficulties I'm asking you to do the same. Let God into any pain you may be facing.

Now, her third son, Levi, is born. Levi seems a breakthrough for Leah's self-image and her being loved by Jacob. Levi means "attached." She said now this time *my husband will become* **attached to me, because I have born him three sons**. The word attach implies to twine, remain or cleave. This appears to be more than just their being legally united in marriage but rather cleaving to one another in heart, affection and attraction. She makes a confident declaration that her husband desires her in ways he had not before. She's beginning to see herself differently. Out of the abundance of her heart, Leah's mouth is now speaking the change that is transpiring inside of her.

Her fourth son is Judah, which means "praise." Over the joy of what God has done for her, Leah says, *"Now I will* **praise the Lord***!"* She's overwhelmed at the hand of God on her life and the change within her own personality. This is a beautiful culmination of God's transforming work in, upon and through Leah. She names her son Praise. She then offers to God praise. It seems, in many ways, Leah is the one God has made to be praised publicly.

"Charm is deceptive, and beauty does not last; but a woman who fears the LORD will be greatly praised. Reward her for all she has done. Let her deeds publicly declare her praise." (Proverbs 31:30-31, NLT)

Leah's fear of the Lord made her to be admired. God's praise upon her life became a greater influence than looks alone. It ultimately made her attractive to Jacob. Praise also means to shine and to be "celebrated." Now, the once re-proached Leah is celebrated by God and the effects are very noticeable. That's what we're talking about here. Not only is Jacob's heart changed toward her, but even Rachel sees how Leah is celebrated to the degree that she becomes envious (Genesis 30:1-2).

You may not feel wanted, but God's favor on your life can make you at-tractive, desirable and loved. Please believe me when I tell you this. I was once an unmarried young adult with a great desire to be married. Your honoring God makes you attractive! God's favor on your life makes you desired. The Anointing can make a young woman physically beautiful. God can make any young woman shine.

When I was eighteen I went with some friends to a special worship service at another church. I remember seeing a girl, about my age, worshipping God with so much freedom and genuine passion: it really amazed me. Listen, on the outside, most would have judged her to be rather plain. But I was so moved watching her worship that it made her extremely physically attractive to me. If you feel like plain Jane, God can make you look desirable. God can make you feel desirable. God made you desirable.

Let me encourage you to fear the Lord. Let Him make you His praise, first. No other guy can establish your worth, so don't let them. Honor the Lord. Be a worshipper. Let Him in to any unlovely part of your heart. He will transform it with favor like He did for Leah and make you shine on the outside. God will make you take a young man's breath away.

You are Responsible

Know that if you honor the Lord, He will honor you. If you praise the Lord with your life, then He will make you His praise (Jeremiah 33:9). He will make you shine and increase your stock price. He will lift you high when you humble yourself in His sight. Without fail, He will promote you when you honor Him. God specializes with making swans from so-called ugly ducklings. My question is, what are you going to do now that *you're all that* for Jesus? Let me help answer that: be responsible to honor the Lord and steward His favor on your life.

In Dress: Remember, God has given you physical beauty. The brothers are sexually attracted to you. Be respectful in what you are wearing. Since a young man is your brother in Christ, don't wear clothes that will be a constant beating on his fragile hormones. Your physical, curvy body is a glory from God to you. Again, you have a powerful influence. The Bible calls the influence of your body on a man as intoxicating. Be very mindful to steward your body by stewarding your attire. If you're 5'11" there's not too much you can do to hide your long legs but at least you can help the cause through the damage control of not wearing short shorts. These kinds of things can get legalistic really fast, but be responsible. Ask God to give your conscience a Christlike sensitivity. Don't play any control games through your attire. You are His very own glory so steward His glory well.

In Conduct: You are some young man's most valued gift so don't unwrap yourself in any way for someone else through sexual sin. Steward your beauty in your habits and behavior. If you're really struggling in this area and your conduct hasn't been very Christlike and you would like it to be, that's wonderful. You can cultivate your warehouse of honor. Every decision of integrity increases honor. Honor can be felt, is tangible and is a legitimate quality of attraction.

Self-Respect: Honor yourself as God honors you. Respect yourself with that same respect. When you do, others will too, including guys. Many young women are sexually active because they do not respect themselves and therefore seek to be loved, accepted and respected through sex. Once again, honor originates from God. Although there is a strong impulse to earn our approval, gain our sense of self-worth, or obtain our validation from people, God's is the Source and Giver of such virtue. None of us wants to feel or be alone. It isn't good that man be alone. God approves of you. God loves you. God made you special. God made you desirable. God said you were more valuable to Him than the Blood of His Son. God will help you to honor yourself so respect yourself today.

Failure of Male Figures

"*...there is not a man on earth...*" (Genesis 19:31, NASB)

Unfortunately, a male authority figure may have failed you already in your young life. Fathers, pastors, teachers, coaches and other male figures have a profound influence on a young girl. If a man has hurt you in your life, then it is possible that a mistrust of men has been cultivated in your heart. I want to tell you from the bottom of my heart how sorry I am for the unfair pain you have faced from a male. It's not the way it's supposed to be.

This is a terrible and common devilish weapon wielded against young women and their future marriages. If you or your mother has been wounded by men then seeds of mistrust toward men may already be planted. I know this isn't a new revelation but you will one day marry a male. If you have not been healed of that wound, then you may see your future spouse as the male figure that hurt you. For a while you may be so in love that you may not see any of his faults as potential issues. However, one day he may accidentally hurt you and that *male authority figure default pain button* in your heart will be pressed. Many women have walked away from their marriages because a father or a first-husband hurt, abused or betrayed their trust. You will need to be on the look-out for this kind of mistrust. If it's in your heart, then it will surface at the most inopportune time. The enemy of your soul will see to it.

Lot's daughters were constantly disappointed by their father. He didn't stay with the divine connection of Uncle Abraham. He followed the pursuit of wealth by going to what seemed to be a better business opportunity in the plains of Sodom. His own sons-in-law didn't take Lot seriously when he told them about the coming judgment upon the land. He freely offered his very own virgin daughters to be raped, ravished and potentially murdered by the wicked men of Sodom (Genesis 19:8, 14, 16). Absolutely unbelievable and pathetic!

Lot, along with the perverts and gluttons of the land, were the examples of men, husbands and fathers to these two young virgin sisters. They were exposed to men of sexual perversion, dishonor toward women and self-indulgence in Sodom and Gomorrah. They witnessed, and were influenced by, a lack of spiritual leadership, protection and true manhood from their own father, Lot.

Now, their homeland is destroyed because of God's judgment and their mother is dead due to her own issues. Lot and the two sisters are hiding in a cave due to his fear of dwelling in the small town of Zoar. This was yet another example of fear and weakness in Lot's character and another negative influence to which his young daughters were exposed. They had been unprotected, unfathered and consistently let down.

Because of their disillusioned perspective of men these two sisters justify a plan to continue their father's lineage. The older sister gets her dad drunk and has sexual relations with him. The younger sister does the same thing the next night. This was their answer for their father to extend his family line. They both got pregnant and their sons were Ammon and Moab. This is completely insane, yet, it is their completely disillusioned reasoning for this horrible behavior that stands out as profound.

> "*Now the firstborn said to the younger, 'Our father is old, **and there is no man on the earth to come in to us** as is the custom of all the earth. Come, let us make our father drink wine, and we will lie with him, that we may preserve the lineage of our father.'*" (Genesis 19:31-33).

150

It sounds like the older sister honestly thought that all the men in the world were dead and gone. Perhaps she thought they were all killed by the fire and hailing brimstone that only rained upon Sodom and Gomorrah. Maybe the two girls were so isolated their whole lives by untrustworthy men that they assumed all men were like those of Sodom and thereby all victims of God's recent judgment. We know this for sure: these two sisters were never exposed to real and godly men, unless they had some memories of Uncle Abraham.

The statement of the older sister, *"There is no man,"* may have well have been *"There are no real men—you can't trust any of them! We have to take care of ourselves!"*

That's just what they did. They preserved their dad's lineage through incest. This terrible tragedy led to painful repercussions for generations to come. My precious sister, mistrust of men can often lead to sin. Acting out on any form of fear will always lead to disaster. I've often thought that while their dad was paralyzed with fear in the cave, the two sisters could have ran off to find Uncle Abraham. He would have helped them for sure. He could have sent them back to his father's house where Laban, Rebekah, Leah and Rachel eventually came from. Instead, a horrible mess came through a mistrust of men.

No matter how many men may disappoint you or women you know, God can be trusted. He can heal and tenderize your heart once again and then direct you into right relationships. Lot's daughters were failed by the culture of men they were surrounded by, especially their father. However, it didn't mean God could not, or would not, have helped them. For the sake of Abraham alone God would have protected Lot's lineage. He could have easily brought godly husbands in order for these two young women to have children.

Your future husband may confirm your value but he is not the source of it. Although your husband should be like Christ to you, no male figure was ever intended by God to replace Christ in your life. Men are going to make mistakes, but God has some real men in His training camp for future husbands. God won't let just any young guy walk off with you, His precious daughter and treasure.

Recently I was at a family wedding. One of my many beautiful and single nieces was there watching her cousin get married. I walked up to her in her wedding attire and said to her pointedly, respectfully and truthfully, "Not just any young man deserves you!" In the natural it is true for her, but I also felt it was said as God inspired my heart to speak value into her life. He is saying the same thing to you now, "My daughter, not just any young man deserves to have you."

If you're wondering what's taking so long for God's choice for you to show up, God may still be putting on the final touches so he's worthy to have you. Don't say out of mistrust, unbelief and bitterness "*There is no man out there!*"

A Few Good Men are Out There

"*Come with me, and meet a man…*" (John 4:29, GWT)

I love this. Here, the five times married Samaritan woman finally meets a real man! They're out there, sister! Of course, she's talking about Jesus. He is the One you ultimately need to be trusting anyways. Jesus can help heal the mistrust of fallible men. Rest assured, in addition to that healing, God also has some young brothers out there and one of them is reserved for you.

Listen to what God says to discouraged Elijah when he thought there was no more godly people out there, "*I have reserved seven thousand in Israel, all whose knees have not bowed to Baal, and every mouth that has not kissed him*" (1 Kings 19:18). He always has a remnant. God has a special guy out there who doesn't look or act like Lot. Perhaps you haven't met him yet or recognize who it is since he's still squirming in the Refiner's Fire of Your Heavenly Father. He'll be looking mighty fine to you when he comes out golden and buff from God's holy gym of character development. He won't be perfect but he'll be approved by God with a ring to put on your finger.

The devil is a liar and liars are fryers. There's a man of God coming your way.

Tips for the Future

Please don't be desperate:

It just does not go well with a guy. You are already special, desirable and attractive to him. Walk in that godly self-assurance. Don't throw your self-respect into the garbage disposal through desperate behavior. Loose clothing is not attractive. I mean, if you used your creativity you could at least dress in a way that leaves something to his imagination to overcome in his own mind. Your body does not define you. Your body is attractive to him but your whole person is who he is drawn to. I'm telling you that you are valuable. Don't throw that away through desperation.

Leslie Ludy, author of *Sacred Singleness*, says to the girls:

> *"As odd as it may sound, I believe the best way to find a godly marriage partner is to stop hunting for one and instead focus your entire life around Jesus Christ and His priorities. We should never put off God's calling upon our life because we haven't met our man yet."* [4]

This is absolutely the truth. Plus, this kind of right focus is honorable and will attract the kind of men God would have for you as a husband.

Don't wait for Mr. Perfect:

There's no perfect guy out there. Don't pass by a great God-opportunity because he hasn't completed his doctorate yet. Don't get too picky or unrealistic. Some girls I've spoken to want this perfect, buff guy making $100,000 a year. Remember, you want God's choice, not necessarily the guy who seems to be Mr. Perfect.

Please have manners:

Don't burp and fart. If you have brothers at home, don't let your manners reflect theirs. You would blow some guys away. I had three sisters, so I grew up with tampon wrappers in the trash and hairy razors in the shower. Following their four hour hiatus in the restroom with Lysol was the norm for me. But your future guy may not have sisters.

Remember, that special guy might be so enamored by you that he will practically worship the ground you walk on. Talking with your mouth full and acting like Miss Congeniality would be devastating to him. Passing gas and challenging him to a stink bomb brawl would be a deathblow. Preserve his fragile and inexperienced conscience, sister. Act like a lady. In time, perhaps after marriage, he will come to grips that you actually go number two on the toilet like he does. Until then be gentle.

Be who God made you to be but don't be a slob. Clean the kitchen at home. Keep your bedroom organized. Floss and brush. Shave your pits. Wear some Perry Ellis 360 or Channel. If you must, bribe and pay off your little brothers or your dad so they don't tell the guy what you're like at home. Just because your future husband might seem to be a lost cause in the area of hygiene, doesn't mean you have to be. Your manners matter. Seriously.

Love God:

Love God and put Him first in your life. This decision makes you most attractive above all else. A young man would fly from the other side of the world to meet you because of this quality decision to honor God above everything else. There is no need to ever underestimate this fact. He is your first love. He can be trusted. Fearing Him first will cause you to shine brightly. Your future husband will see and be drawn to that light.

Again, as Proverbs 31 says, "*Her children rise up and call her blessed; Her husband also, and he praises her: Many daughters have done well,*

But you excel them all. Charm is deceitful and beauty is passing, But a woman who fears the LORD, she shall be praised. Give her of the fruit of her hands, And let her own works praise her in the gates."

Your time is coming. Stay steady and love God best. Love ya my little sister. You're beautiful. Hang tough!

PRAYER:

"Lord Jesus, please help me to recognize that You made me special and attractive. Help me then also to be responsible and steward this influence in a way that is pleasing to You. I pray that You would give me grace to trust You to bring the right guy into my life, at the right time and in the right way. I want to please You and having Your best in my life pleases You. If there is any mistrust in my heart of males in general I ask that You would purge me of it. May my trust in You first be strengthened. I believe You have my best interests at heart. My steps are ordered of You. In Jesus name, Amen."

Chapter 11

Preparing for "The Right One"
Letting God build Your Dream for Marriage

Recently, a soon to be married girl said emphatically to me as she was describing her beautiful wedding dress, "I've been dreaming of this since I was twelve!" As much as some guys may not want to admit it, he feels the same way. It was an awesome moment when my bride was finally walking down that decorated aisle toward me to become my wife. After all of the years of waiting, this most beautiful twenty one year old was about to be my wife. As I watched her coming toward me with my future father-in-law, I sensed God whisper to my heart, "Here is My gift to you." It's still an awesome thought that in that moment she was going to take my name, become my crown, give herself to me and wear a ring that says I belong to Samuel Beckworth. What a miracle.

Getting married to the person God made for you is a seed of great desire and nearly unexplainable longing planted inside of each and every heart by our Creator. How involved He is in the process! It's really tough to take it all in but it's great to try. Yes, on earth a credentialed minister performs the ceremony and signs the necessary state documents to recognize the two as legally married. But God Himself, from heaven, makes two people one in spirit. He recognizes before all in heaven, on earth and under the earth this most blessed union. Your marrying the one God has prepared specifically for you is one of His greatest dreams for you, too. *Your greatest preparation in marrying that person includes allowing God to build His dream in you.*

Resisting sexual sin takes extreme discipline. Unfortunately, our self-will, as determined as it may be, can't lead us to the promise land of holiness. Only things truly born of God can inspire the kind of discipline that is required to fully obey God. A dream inspires successful discipline. Vision can restrain us from sin (Proverbs 29:18). Joseph's life proves this. Furthermore, passion or delight in a dream will cause you to make present decisions based on that future.

God has a dream for you to marry someday. God is a huge dreamer. He wants you to live the dream. Like anything worthwhile, it takes time and commitment to see the process through. What will keep us on course and steady through those seemingly long years before the dream of marriage comes to pass is the dream itself. Let's take a look at this process:

The Planting of the Dream Seed:

For something to grow a seed must be planted. It probably doesn't take much to recognize the desire to be married. It is His dream He is calling you to dream. It starts here. God has already planted this seed in you.

The Watering of the Dream Seed:

Seeds must be watered. Your dream of marrying *the one* must be watered also. This happens as you commit yourself to the Lord's process and way of bringing the right person into your life. This watering may come in the form of an experience, like a moment of truth, when you are deeply touched by God to acknowledge and pursue His best concerning this part of your life.

This happened for me, in part, when I attended the *Why Wait?* seminar. For me I knew I wanted to honor God by resisting sexual sin and marry the right person. This is where the dream seed is watered, breaks open and comes alive in you. Your responsibility is to seek God with your whole heart.

CHAPTER 11

"Trust in the Lord with all your heart, and lean not on your own understanding; In all your ways acknowledge Him, and He shall direct your paths." (Proverbs 3:5-6)

Dream-based Decisions:

Every decision of integrity you choose to sow is a seed toward building your future dream. Every sacrificial choice you make now that is consistent with God's best for your life down the road will grow the dream in you. When you say no to going on a date with someone you know you should not go out with, even though you might fight loneliness, it will add life and growth to the dream. The expectation for your future spouse and the passion to settle for nothing less than God's best will come alive in you, like a woman with a child in her womb. Every time you say yes to God and no to compromising relationships, the dream in you grows. As the dream for *the one* forms in you then give your highest attention to make present decisions based on that dream!

Before I was married I stopped looking too long at women and commenting inappropriately. I would not do that if I was married so I chose not to do that even before I was married. I knew I would lead my wife and future family after I was married so I started leading myself spiritually through daily Bible reading, fasting and prayer, being connected to the local church and tithing before I was married. What would you do or not do after you meet and marry *the right one*? Well, get started or stop it right now! This is what faith does. It acts in advance of the promise.

I remember being in a church service when my future wife walked right in front of me taking her seat in the church service. We were not dating at the time, but by then I was made aware that she wanted to get to know me more. I was still in the refusing to date mode. As she walked in front of me, although I was aware of her and how attractive she was in form and appearance, I didn't look. I kept my eyes on the multi-media screen and continued worshipping. I was not aware of it but my future father-in-law was watching me from the other side of that large worship center. He was impressed to say the least that I wasn't distracted by looking at her during worship. Every other guy she ever walked by seemed to fall over like a domino. He knew I was different. Why? I was *the one* and God expected me to act like I was *the one* for someone.

Thankfully, it is much easier to make the sacrificial decisions as the dream grows larger in you. Make right decisions and the dream in you grows. As the dream grows it is easier to make right decisions that are consistent with the dream.

Build While You Battle:

We've established that you'll need to be in battle mode in this season of your life. Sexual temptation demands you stay on your guard. At the same time God will also be building and rebuilding some part of your life. I doubt you're perfect and imagine you may have some junk in your life that needs to get cleaned up. Young people have brokenness God will help heal during this time. If you've had sex once or even allowed petting, if you've been abused, if you had a pain in the neck teacher as a kid or if your dad spoke careless words to you as a five year old, then you'll need some healing.

Young people carry drama and baggage into their potential marriage relationship that will rear its ugly head at the most inopportune time and just about send that other person running. God will use this dream time to help rebuild you while you battle.

This is what the great story concerning the book and person of Nehemiah is all about. God gave this tremendous leader a mission to rebuild the wall of Jerusalem. After the destruction of Jerusalem by the Chaldeans, God began drawing His people back to inhabit Jerusalem once again some 70 seventy later. First, the temple was built. Now it was time for the walls around the city to be rebuilt to offer protection to the inhabitants of the city and the temple. The enemies of the Jews were furious and constantly threatened God's people with manipulation and fear tactics.

The rebuilding of the wall was a major undertaking and required some serious focus and a little multi-tasking. The mission was to build the wall but unless the labor force was aware of their enemy then their mission would be sabotaged and they would probably be killed. Solving the challenge, Nehemiah, one of the greatest leaders in the entire Bible, instructed them so that "*with one hand they worked at construction, and with the other held a weapon*" (Nehemiah 4:17).

You have a mission to fulfill: it's called Y2S JNY: *Yes to Sex... Just Not Yet!* To eventually live in the reality of this dream, you have to constantly carry your weapons of warfare and wear your armor while you allow the Lord to rebuild you. You are God's workmanship (Ephesians 2:10). You are God's handiwork. His two edged Sword is not just for the devil's intestines, it's also for our own soul.

> "*For the Word that God speaks is alive and full of power [making it active, operative, energizing, and effective]; it is sharper than any two-edged sword, penetrating to the dividing line of the breath of life (soul) and [the immortal] spirit, and of joints and marrow [of the deepest parts of our nature], exposing and sifting and analyzing and judging the very thoughts and purposes of the heart. And not a creature exists that is concealed from His sight, but all things are open and exposed, naked and defenseless to the eyes of Him with Whom we have to do.*" (Hebrews 4:11-13, AMP)

Wow. That's a mouthful. Sorry to say, but you might be a little more like Shrek on the inside than you realize and need the layers of the onion peeled away. Although Jesus legally destroyed sin and death, we still have the responsibility to appropriate what He did for us. Our minds need to be renewed by the Word of God. Rebuilding the wall is a parallel to rebuilding the wall of our soul. You may already be born again in the same way the temple was already rebuilt in Jerusalem. But unless the walls of our soul are built then we can live

161

in fear and inferiority just like the Jews did in the days of Nehemiah. Let God help you build while you battle. Look for these opportunities for healing and wholeness from your past.

Any gap in the wall of your soul is a breach and opening for the enemy of your soul to take advantage. Fear was a major open door in the famous story of Job. God was not Job's problem, fear was. Don't let the enemy take advantage of your weakness. Let Jesus in as He knocks on the door of your heart to reveal and heal any part of your heart He sees fit. Your Father, the Master Builder, always and only has your freedom and best in mind.

As your personal wholeness increases, you will sense a greater depth and maturity taking place in you. You will also sense the Lord's hand in preparing you to actually become a husband to one of His precious daughters or a wife to one of His sons. Do not waste this precious time. You'll never get it back. Build while you battle.

Cry While You Die:

Let's be honest, it hurts when others are off getting hitched and you're not. It's painful when 'Sister Christian' is off having sex with the football team and not waiting for 'Brother Christian' who is trying his best to wait for her. It's tough for the girls who outnumber the guys 7 to 1, especially when the guys aren't stepping up to the plate. It just gets old and you have to continue to fight against what appears to be an eternal discouragement. The temptation will be to just give up and say 'enough of this!' But dreamers must continue to get up again on the inside. We're not foolish for continuing to persevere and believe. This is the victory that overcomes the world, even our faith.

So why does it hurt so much? This pain you're feeling is your lower nature facing a slow death.

1 Peter 4:1 says, *"Whoever has suffered in the flesh [having the mind of Christ]…[has stopped pleasing himself and the world, and pleases God]."* (AMP)

Your suffering in the flesh is an awesome sign. Don't be afraid of this kind of pain. Eat it for breakfast. It simply speaks loudly of your refusal to live for yourself but instead for Him. Your suffering is found in the resisting of intentional sin. Refusing to please yourself and forcing your lower nature into its proper place of submission is where the true Biblical suffering of the believer lies. I know it flat out hurts sometimes, but know for certain you are pleasing God. Go ahead and cry when necessary. You're not sinning for doing this, unless it rolls into a self-centered pity-party. But when you're finished shedding some tears, wash off your face and stand tall.

I love this passage in Hebrews 11:35. It says of some of the heroes of faith that they *"were tortured, not accepting deliverance, that they might obtain a better resurrection."* Your better resurrection, promotion and dream are coming in the morning. Promotion doesn't come from the east or the west but from the Lord. You might be genuinely disappointed at what is happening around you but your destiny and greatness is born of God, is being nurtured and brought to pass by God. Trust Him. Hang tough if right now you're crying because your flesh is dying because God isn't lying. It is critical for the life of the dream growing inside of your spiritual womb.

Whistle While You Work:

*"**Trust** in the LORD, and do good; **Dwell** in the land and cultivate faithfulness. **Delight yourself** in the LORD; And He will give you the desires of your heart. **Commit** your way to the LORD, **Trust** also in Him, and **He will do it**."* (Psalm 37:3-5, NASB)

This is where you get lost in the dream, through thanksgiving. In the natural *the one* may not appear to be any closer to coming into your life than last year.

163

However a real miracle is taking place inside of you. Somehow, trust in God is increasing in you and a calm sense of faith will slowly replace the anxiety of whether, or not, *the one* will ever show up. Somehow when a part of your lower nature dies due to obedience, another part of your new nature comes to life.

In the Kingdom of God resurrection life follows death. When you give up something of yourself, something of God rises up within you. You actually begin to believe God can bring your future spouse to you no matter the circumstances.

Delight yourself in the Lord when it looks like nothing is happening. Trust, do good, cultivate faithfulness and commit your way to Him with joy *before* your change comes. God will keep you busy with the joy of your heart. It's great compensation while the desire of your heart nears your door.

Refuse Self-promotion:

Force yourself to only accept promotion from the Lord. You would rather be unmarried for the rest of your life than to do this thing your way and force a relationship into existence. What?! If you don't believe me just look around and ask some questions from people who rushed the process. Make it your position that your dream or "*exaltation comes neither from the east nor from the west nor from the south. But God is the Judge: He puts down one, and exalts another*" (Psalm 75:6-7). Since your marriage partner is one of the greatest promotions you will ever receive, make sure this promotion is coming from God and not you.

I remember going witnessing with our young adult group when I was 19. One of the girls in the group wanted us to date. She was a great gal but a bit forward assuming I was all for it. She wasn't a bad looking chick. She loved God, was faithful in her church, a tither and also had long legs. Most of all she was Mexican, which would have won over my East Los Angeles relatives. There was only one problem. There was no green light from God. He said nothing different from our mutual 'no date' conviction. Therefore there was not even a second thought. No date for Sammy and *chica*, end of story. She ended up getting ticked off about it. Listen closely, I can't tell you how much I didn't care.

After all, who can find a virtuous wife? Who can find that young man of honor? God can so refuse self-promotion.

Dream in the Direction of the Rewarder:

"But without faith it is impossible to please Him, for he who comes to God must believe that He is, and that He is a rewarder of those who diligently seek Him." (Hebrews 11:6)

Setting aside all spiritual hype, I eventually became convinced that God could bring my wife to me from anywhere in the world. Therefore I had no need, and even refused, to look for her. *"Who can find a virtuous wife?"* Proverbs asks, with no apparent answer. I wrote in response in my old Bible when I was twenty, *"God can!"* I didn't need and would have no part in trying to track her down. I'm not saying that's where you need to live but I became full of that passion. I'm not telling you how to approach it but that was just the way I rolled.

I remember a conversation I was having with my pastor's sister. She was one of the nicest and caring people I ever knew. She loved my future wife and knew she was interested in dating. She felt like I should prayerfully consider whether I should pursue getting to know Kim more. She was completely respectful in her nudging me in Kim's direction. It was almost in a playful way like, "Hey, Kim likes you! What do you think?" I practically yelled out in response, "God knows where I am. God knows where my future wife is. God knows how to bring us together! He doesn't need my help!" I totally overwhelmed this poor lady.

Yes, I overreacted somewhat. I never meant to be hurtful or rude. I was just full of conviction and refused to allow even a little influence that could lead to my orchestrating this part of my life. I was dreaming in the direction of the Rewarder of my faith. God alone was going to bring this to pass in my life. Don't forget: believe that God is a rewarder of those who diligently seek Him!

Loving the Dream Giver more than the Dream:

Again, I truly believed that God did not want me to date after I committed my heart completely to Him at age 18. This three year test had its tough moments. Then I met my future wife. After meeting Kim, she wanted to go out with me for ten months. She was beautiful, very attractive and very in love with God. I was flattered. I was a stud at 6'2", weighing in at 160 pounds, soaking wet. If my half Mexican head wasn't so big, I think I would have weighed 140.

However, although my convictions on dating did not change, I felt some things began to change inside my heart. They were changing inside of Kim's heart too. I heard through the gospel grapevine she was tired of waiting around for me. In my reasoning, it seemed that if I didn't make a move then she was going to move on. I thought, "Here we go again... another pretty girl who loves God slipping through my fingers. Will this relationship thing ever happen for me?"

You see, I knew that if I asked Kim on a date in a panic or in an effort to keep her in my back pocket that it would have been wrong. I would have replaced God as the architect of my future. Once again, I knew I had to let go. I could not take control of any relationship and keep God in control of my life at the same time.

Although I had been firm on the same conviction for three years it was all coming to a head. It was as if I came to this realization that I might never get married. It may sound silly to say but for me that possibility became so real that I knew I was facing the most painful and sobering moment of truth in my life: I might be like the Apostle Paul and never marry. This could be my calling. It was so real at the time. I bawled my head off. I had never fought such feelings of potential loneliness and abandonment in my whole life until that point. As Buddy the Elf said of the mailroom tube, it was, "Very sucky!"

Nevertheless, I chose to stir myself up. I was just about dead to myself by that time anyways, so I decided to go all the way with God. Resolved, I stood up and told God that "if it never happens, if I never get married, You will always be my first love!" I wept some more with a deep sense of His love and resolve in my heart. Then in charismatic fashion I boldly danced before the Lord with all of my strength and praised Him with all of my heart. I did not care what the price was. It was all out on the line. It was the nail in the coffin in refusing to promote myself. To this day I remember exactly where I was and what that experience felt like over 17 years ago.

Perhaps you, too, fight these feelings or are facing this very sobering possibility. Please be encouraged that by this experience God allowed me to see that I chose to love God more than my desire to be married. You too may be tested to the max to love the Dream Giver more than the dreams He gives us. Maybe not. You honestly may not have to face this. For me this was my final test before God presented my future wife to me.

The Dream Becomes your Reality:

*"Remember those early days after you first saw the light? Those were the hard times! So don't throw it all away now. You were sure of yourselves then. It's still a sure thing! But you need to stick it out, staying with God's plan so you'll be there for the promised completion. It won't be long now, he's on the way; **he'll show up most any minute.**"* (Hebrews 10:32, 35-37, MESSAGE)

Two weeks after that moment of truth experience the dream became a reality. Here's how it went down.

I asked Kim if she would take an evening with me to get some coffee to talk. I explained to her my heart in why I had chosen not to date and continued not to date. As we spent some time getting to know each other a little more, I went into my whole spiel. I explained why I felt God didn't want me to date unless He made it undeniably clear. It needed to be like *Back to the Future*: Darth Vader threatening to 'melt my brain if I didn't ask Lorraine to the enchantment under the Sea Dance.' We had a very nice and pleasant time together. She really respected where I was coming from. Later, she told me how much it impressed her and made her like me even more.

It also was very good for me to spend time with her that evening since I never even gave myself a chance to really get to know her. Well, in the middle of my talking to her that night something began to happen. While looking at her while she was talking, my whole heart fluttered. *Oh snap*! In my mind I immediately yelled, "What the heck was that Lord?! You have some explaining to do!" I mean, here I was explaining to her why I wasn't going to ask her out on a date and then my heart flutters over her right in the middle of my *holy things* talk! I tried to ignore it for the moment and continued with our evening.

After praying later about my "heart flutter by Kim," I really didn't know what to think as I was beyond my comfort zone. God was silent but I could feel that things were changing inside of me fast. I was getting major nervous as I knew there were some uncharted feelings going on inside of me. I didn't know what to do with them, but I did know that my heart was in God's hands and I could trust Him. What I soon found out was that Darth Vader was about to threaten to melt my brain.

Within that two week period, our church hosted a special guest speaker. As I walked into the worship center that evening and was preparing to find my seat, there she was. Kim was standing there just smiling at me. I can describe with vivid clarity what she was wearing, her smile and her tan. She physically took my breath away. Those three seconds she looked at me affectionately with her beautiful smile felt like one full minute.

In that moment, God removed a veil from my eyes and showed me beyond any doubt that I was to break my three year fast and ask Kim on a date. She knew on our first date I was her future husband. I knew after two months she was my wife. We married a year and a half after our first date.

One fine day, she showed up. One fine day, he's going to want you for his girl. One day your whole life changes when your future spouse comes into your life. One day your dream will become a reality. You will never be the same. It really will happen. It is a dream come true. Be there when it does and "*stick it out so you'll be there for the promised completion.*"

PRAYER:

"*Heavenly Father, I want to be a dreamer like You. Help me to see the bigger picture. Help me to live and make decisions according to that master blueprint You've designed specifically for my life. I receive the substance of real Bible faith to add form, growth and increase to Your seed of marriage within me. I receive in advance the promise of the dream becoming reality for me. You're first in my life Lord. May it always be this way. In Jesus name I pray, Amen.*"

Chapter 12

A Word to The Presently Engaged:
Finish Your Race Well

Our Engagement Picture

W hat a most special time of life you're in right now. It is truly a gift. You are at the threshold of a very special finish line: One that brings an end to one race and also a beginning to a new one.

"Endings are better than beginnings." (Ecclesiastes 7:8, MESSAGE)

This passage isn't quite the choice or theme marriage Scripture but in a way it describes the finish line ahead as your wedding day approaches. Obviously this chapter is highlighting the beginning of marriage, and rightfully so. But I want you for a moment to reflect on what is ending—the unwed life.

During your single years, I'm sure there were questions, pain, frustration, doubts and loneliness: "Will I ever find the right guy" or "Will I ever have what it takes to be a real man?" But it's been during these times that you've allowed Jesus to make the difference and to walk that journey with you throughout those years. Now, He has faithfully brought you to this very special place of engagement. Remember and cherish those times when it was just you and Jesus. It has made you who you are today and they will serve as a godly testimony to others who are still on their journey.

Although being engaged is not without its probable challenges, God wants you to thoroughly enjoy every bit of this season. Temper any anxiety you may be feeling as you approach your wedding date with a greater perspective. This season of your life is coming to a close. I would like to share just a few thoughts that could be a help and encourage you to finish your race of the single life well.

Enjoy the Ride

You are about to leave the single life after a lot of years. A beautiful and miraculous transition awaits you. You're going to be married soon. It is one of the most thrilling emotions of excitement you will ever experience. Let me then also encourage you to cherish the remainder of your special time of engagement. Soak in what God has been to you while single. Absorb every special blessing that comes. Breathe in this change of life and how God is presently gracing you for the married life.

Don't be in such a rush for that wedding date to hit the calendar that you're not taking in the excitement all around you right now. Allow yourself to live in the moment, seize the day, and enjoy the ride. Even in the midst of the stress of wedding preparation, recognize the beauty of what's taking place. Ten years will pass by right in front of your eyes. By God's grace you will never experience this season of your life again. It's a special gift.

Within three weeks of my first date with Kim, I was completely and totally in love. I slipped into a realm of near stupor. Song of Solomon 5:8 said, "*I am lovesick*"; and I was for sure. I had never experienced these powerful feelings for anyone in my life so I was in uncharted and unfamiliar territory. For years I was the *no date-no feel Nazi* and now it was like the carpet of the norm was being stripped by God Himself right from under my feet. I didn't know what to do or what to make of it.

After two months, it was beyond my control and it scared me a little bit. I really wanted God's help and as I prayed about my new pathetic condition I was impressed with these words, "*enjoy the ride.*" Simultaneously I saw this picture in my heart of a big water-slide like you would find at one of the big water parks. The water was flowing down the slide just like it was supposed to. With my new found intoxication for my future wife I was to jump on the water slide and enjoy the adventure.

No work. No struggle. No striving. Just be doused with His blessing of Kim in my life. I believe God impressed these words and image in my heart to release my joy and emotions into this beautiful experience of falling in love with my future wife. My human tendency was to clamp down, grit my teeth and plow ahead! *No time to enjoy life—there are more important Kingdom issues to contend with!* Obviously that is silly. God wants you deeply happy.

> Jesus "*came that they may have and enjoy life, and have it in abundance (to the full, till it overflows).*" (John 10:10, AMP)

Man, I got wound up for those three years so God had to take His time to unwind me. When we are on a stricter mission that requires more discipline we can easily get overly caught up in our works rather than the grace of God. For me the fight of waiting for *the one* was over, but I was still swinging like the boxing match was still going on. I was still too intense and yet everything in life will always be a grace thing when God is in it.

I had to get out of the mode of the prior season and fall completely into the new season. God so much wanted me to enjoy it, which is why I believe He helped me that day. He loosened me up and I lost control in a good way. I was defeated by the lovesick potion of Almighty God and I was happy to lose that battle. Enjoy the ride.

Stay Smart

"Let your eyes look straight ahead, and your eyelids look right before you. Ponder the path of your feet, and let all your ways be established. Do not turn to the right or the left; Remove your foot from evil." (Proverbs 4:25-27)

Although God may help you bring down some necessary walls during this engagement season He still wants you to keep up your guard against enemies. The devil likes to play the role of the spoiler. A spoiler in sports is when a team who is out of playoff contention beats a team who is in contention thereby spoiling their chances to make the post season. The devil and his team aren't making it to the playoffs. You, on the other hand, are going to the playoffs of marriage and your enemy wants to spoil it. He would love to trip you up just before sprinting through to the finish line. He wants to separate, weaken or at least reproach what God is joining together through you and your future spouse. He will use things in your past you're not proud of or attempt to spoil your relationship through sexual sin or any other kind of drama he could get his hands on.

Remember, no cleavage until you leave-age. Stay on your guard. Don't start making out like crazy simply because you're only one month away. Don't start praying together and laying together. Don't start "Facebooking" all your ex-girlfriends or boyfriends. The enemy may not be able to defeat you head on so he'll try to trip you from behind. Stay smart. You've come a long way. Keep leaning on your Master.

> *"For the LORD will be your confidence, and will keep your foot from being caught."* (Proverbs 3:26)

Stay focused. Keep loving God and being obedient. Get up quickly if you stumble. The enemy is still the loser. You are the winner. Just stay the course, finish it out and see it through.

Keep Peddling

There will be challenges during the engagement period. Some of them come from without: *a bride-to-be's mother wanting to control all of the aspects of her daughter's wedding.* Some come from within: *a young future groom who is facing the greatest fears of his life as he wonders if he has what it takes to be a husband and a provider. Am I a real man?* When facing discouragement, inferiority and insecurity keep moving forward.

There may be all kinds of pressures that attempt to directly challenge your future marriage but all that truly matters is whether or not God was the orchestrator of your joining. Sure, there are many things to consider like career, finances, education and wedding details. First, I trust you've included godly counsel to help determine whether this person is your future mate. Don't be overly confident that you're mature enough at an early age to say, "God said" they're my future spouse. So, assuming you've secured wisdom for marriage through godly counsel, you should continue with that counsel through your days of engagement. Your parents, pastor, mentors and trusted friends should know your strengths and weaknesses, be allowed to speak into your life and perhaps even help with some of the practical details of your future together.

Yet when the dust settles and all signs are a go to be married, don't allow the pressures before that wedding day to make you double minded. Don't start changing the wedding date because you're facing some fear. Don't start saying foolish things out of your emotions and let your insecurities motivate your actions. Don't start pulling back saying you're not ready. I'll tell you right now you're not ready! In many ways you don't have what it takes, have enough money or are mature enough. But if God says you're ready then you're ready.

He's looking at your heart. God can make you what you're not. God can give you more money. God can bring you to a greater place of character and maturity. His grace is sufficient for you. He just needs your teachable and surrendered heart. Now, be bold and keep moving forward.

Three months into our relationship it was settled we were going to be married. It was the Lord's doing and it was marvelous in our eyes. I had only one problem: I had no job, no money, no BA degree and no car.

At the time I was working in full time youth ministry for a church and my only compensation was paid living expenses. That was great especially since we believed that ministry was going to be a major part of our future. However, I knew that this was not going to last forever and that some things were going to have to change soon. Eventually, Kim was going to wonder, "Okay dude, so how are we going to live financially once we're married?" Living on love ain't going to do it.

Over the next several months I began to progressively face growing insecurities and inferiority that truly challenged whether I was ready to marry. I was not feeling like a knight in shining armor, if you know what I mean. I was facing some serious doubts about whether I was man enough to be a husband and provider. Economically I did not grow up in an affluent or even a middle class home. As a kid, my idea of being rich was to eat the real General Mills Coco Puffs instead of the sorry Malt-O-Meal brands. I wanted to pour my cereal from a box instead of a stinking bag! We had to eat sorry discounted Maizoro corn flakes with the busted up box that was sold on the bottom shelf! My parents had seven children and my mom stayed home with us. We just didn't have a lot of things.

Well, I believe I carried some shame from my childhood into my adulthood and it suddenly culminated into an intense battle. I really began to feel like two people. The struggle only grew worse but it was God's way of bringing this stuff to the surface. Several months into our engagement, it all began to come to a head and I didn't know if I could take it anymore. At times I genuinely wondered if the whole thing needed to be called off. I started entertaining negative thoughts of failure, not being good enough for Kim and being a second rate man.

Thank God I was trained to know the power of my words and was careful not to speak these things out in a careless way. At first I thought I somehow opened a door to the enemy to harass me because this seemed to come out of nowhere, but that wasn't the case. As it turned out, there were some deeper issues within my heart that went far beyond having a lack of money. God was allowing these fears to come to the surface. I realized that it wasn't the devil attacking me so much as God drawing out a lot of ugly stuff that was already in me for a long time. Sure the enemy wanted to capitalize on this but in the bigger picture I was in the Refiner's Fire and it was getting hot in God's kitchen.

So here I was, at the peak of this fiery trial challenging my destiny with Kim. With no car, I got on my bike to go to Kim's house to spend time with her and her family. My fiancé was without a doubt the cream of the crop, in every way, out of all the young women in the large church she attended. Her father was an elder and a man of reputation and standing in the community through his career with the third largest gas utility company in the country. Here I am: their daughter's knight and shining armor picking her up on my mountain bike for a fancy dinner at Taco Bell while fighting off images of Pee Wee Herman in my mind. With each pedal, I was fighting the devil's trash talk, plus all of these emotions at their peak. I had no food. I had no job. My pets' heads were falling off!

Well, I remember vividly coming to a stop sign with still twenty minutes to go to get to her house. I stopped, put my head down and sighed deeply, feeling all of the weight of this vicious discouragement. I felt like I couldn't take this battle against insecurity anymore. It was at that moment I heard the Lord's voice deep inside my heart say something I will never forget, *"Just keep peddling."*

To this day those words are still awesome to me. God was not just telling me to keep riding my bike to Kim's house to enjoy the afternoon with her and her family. God was in reality telling me to keep moving in the direction of my destiny and future and He would help me sort of the rest. Just keep peddling and obey and I'll make your crooked places straight and crooked brain straighten out. Just keep peddling and move in the direction of the dream and I'll bless you. Just keep peddling in your heart toward destiny and eventually you won't be peddling on a bike to Kim's house.

When I heard those words a deeper influence than discouragement began to rise up inside of me. I entered yet another level of personal resolve and more importantly a more mature trust in Him. I soon picked up my head and shook off as much of that discouraging junk as I possibly could and kept peddling to Kim's house that afternoon. Any insecurity that tried to linger was just going to have to be dragged along for the ride if it could endure it because I wasn't stopping. After all, that's a big part of the life of faith. If God was big enough to get me to this point in my life, He was big enough to get me to the finish line. I rebuked that trash talking loud mouth, too:

> "*No weapon forged against you will prevail, and* **you will refute every tongue that accuses you**. *This is the heritage of the servants of the LORD, and this is their vindication from me,*" *declares the LORD.*" (Isaiah 54:17, NIV)

Within a few short months I had a cool car completely paid for, solid jobs with steady income and the blessings haven't stopped since. There are a lot of different challenges that can be overcome by continuing to peddle. When you're in the will of God doing the best you know to do, stay on course. Keep moving forward. Prove your faith by doing. When it's hard, just keep peddling. Through your heartfelt obedience, God is doing more in you and for you than you can presently imagine. You'll be eating the fruit of it for the rest of your life.

Our Wedding Picture

Congratulations. May your engagement time be rich. May your wedding day be graced by His Presence. May your marriage be blessed.

PRAYER:

Heavenly Father, I want to finish this race with excellence. Help me to continue to walk in holiness and take in all the great things You're doing in my life. While enjoying this time with my future spouse help me to stay focused. Strengthen me to continue to keep peddlin' through any and all circumstances facing me on the outside and through any fears I'm struggling with on the inside. In all things You have made me more than a conqueror. You truly are the Author and the Finisher of my faith. I am so thankful You have brought me to this place in my life. You have been and still are so faithful to me. Be glorified in me, my future spouse and my marriage to come. Thank you for everything. In the wonderful name of Jesus I pray, Amen!

Chapter 13

Speaking to the Gay Sex Issue
Gaining a Christlike Perspective

It would be wrong and a disservice to you, the reader, to have a book like this in your hands and not have the subject of gay sex mentioned. Actually, in our present culture, homosexuality both demands and deserves much more than a mention. It requires an honest conversation filled with grace and truth, wrapped in God's loving compassion. God is always right and always does things right. In His day they said of Jesus, "He does all things well." We who represent Jesus need His help to do the same. Unfortunately, concerning gays, it is no secret that the Body of Christ has much room for improvement.

The issue of gay sex, or the homosexual lifestyle, isn't so much about a topic or a doctrine as much as it is about a person. It is the person, the individual, God values and pursues. Someone who chooses to act on same-sex impulses is of no less value to God, nor any less loved. The Lord is not an insecure Father who is more indignant about His laws than He is *in love* with people. In fact, the Father of all spirits implemented His laws in order to facilitate and enhance relationship with Him and others.

The person in a gay lifestyle, or one struggling with same-sex attractions, is not repulsive to God. God wants people free and blessed. The Lord knows that sexual sin, including homosexual interaction, does not liberate people. But Jesus does:

"It is for freedom that Christ has set us free." (Galatians 5:1, NIV)

181

Although God's great expectations for us include holiness, we also see that His unchanging Word is for our benefit and not for our detriment; for our protection and not harm; to establish healthy boundaries for our good and not to control us; to release us into purpose and not to restrict us; to bring us abundant life and not misery. James, the half brother of Jesus, called the Scriptures *the perfect law of liberty*, not *the overbearing law of bondage*. God's grand desire is not to rule you with an iron fist. God is not looking down on you in a condescending way, holding the 10 Commandments over your head to intimidate you or to "teach you a lesson" or to "show you who's boss." The devil is the liar here. He is the one that coerces people into the iron furnace and tries to turn around and blame God for his garbage. On the contrary, God is for you more than you know.

Again, the Scriptures point the way to our most deeply satisfying life. This perhaps is one of the reasons His principles have never and will never change. For God to alter His laws to fit a changing and compromising culture would equate to God altering and compromising His love for you and me. Thankfully, God the Father is the perfect parent and will not alter His Word or His love.

Besides, God knows you better than you know yourself. God knows what will bless you more than you do. Father truly knows best. Let's see what He has to say.

Gay Sex Experimentation

As we already covered in chapter two, any sexual activity outside of marriage between a man and a woman is sin. Porneia, the Greek word for sexual immorality, is any sex sin outside of God's original intent. It includes anything from masturbation to porn to petting to intercourse, and also, same-sex experimentation.

Since it is not okay to experiment with opposite-gender sex, it is also not okay to fool around with gay sex. We are instructed to flee all forms of sexual immorality. It's important to be clear that God's perspective on same-gender sex is not foggy from the plumb line of the eternal Scriptures.

It is the act of homosexuality that God condemns. The person is not detestable, vile, degrading or shameful. The sin is (Genesis 19:1-13, Leviticus 20:13, 1 Corinthians 6:9-11). If you have homosexual struggles, or love someone who does, please understand this: Homosexual behavior is not the unforgivable sin. It is one sin in a long list of things that are outside of His will.

Many good young people who have experimented, and yet desire to pursue a godly opposite-sex relationship, are struggling to pull away from same-sex attractions.

If this is you, or if you're pressured to experiment, I would first ask you not to do so. Invite Jesus to tell you who you are. If you've already experimented and are presently struggling to get out of or stay away from these attractions, I hope to encourage you. Your feelings or impulses do not define your identity. My prayer is that the Lord would direct you to the right people to help you through this journey to be all God made you to be.

Don't allow the confused culture we live in to be the dominating voice of influence in your life. The world is messed up. You don't want what they have. You were made to soar. May God unleash the real you!

Also, please understand that God's love for you does not change if you choose same-sex relationships. God values you greatly regardless of your potential choice to live outside of His original intent for sex. Since this love issue is settled then, allow me to make another point: Sin will still destroy you even though God loves you. Don't buy the lie that "since God loves me no matter what then it's okay for me to have gay sex." Sin is always damaging.

There is also a misunderstanding that "if you really loved gays then you would also support the lifestyle." Do not confuse loving and respecting a person to mean you are to condone a lifestyle that is outside the boundaries of Scripture. James said that all men were made in the image of God (James 3:9). Peter said we are to "honor all people" (1 Peter 2:17). A person's conduct will never alter their intrinsic value and distinct worth before God and man. Therefore, there's no reason for a heterosexual Christian to feel threatened, insecure or uncomfortable when they find themselves around someone who is gay. Show honor and speak blessing! God have mercy on the church for our failures in this area. Yet, our love and support for the *person* does not equate to affirming the *conduct*. God calls us to both value the person and also align ourselves with Bible truth concerning the boundaries of sex as God intended.

Obviously, there's a whole lot more to the issue, but the truth being emphasized here is simple. Same-gender sex is sin and you should stay away from it. I realize that's a plain statement but not too many people are saying it plain anymore. The fruit of this failure has been the terrible confusion that pervades this present youth culture.

Same-Sex Culture

This present evil age is in a mad rush to persuade young people that same-sex experimentation may be required for one to search out their real identity and find their true self.

Recently, a friend's twin daughters were exposed to this way of thinking at their high school. The Health Science teacher introduced his freshman class to a gay man and a lesbian. The teacher allowed the two homosexuals to express their perspective to the students. His girls felt very uncomfortable by the pressure they felt, from the speakers and their teacher, to be open to this lifestyle for themselves. There was also no advance warning given to the parents or students concerning the class agenda for that particular day.

The teacher also spoke in a derogatory tone toward parental authority as he knew some parents were steering their children away from homosexuality. Obviously my friend was not very happy, to say the least.

Although this kind of conduct is no longer a surprise, this sway of influence is something to be very aware of. Christian or not, conservative or liberal, gay or straight, I think most would agree that the culture around us is shifting. There is a spiritual and moral climate change of vast proportions in our nation.

This shift is tangible in public opinion, the news, sitcoms, in our state and federal governments, and even, now, in the legislation of laws. This same-sex culture push is acute, intentional and growing more bold as the days pass and as each election comes and goes. Unfortunately, in regard to morality and spirituality, what was once ignored generations ago by the church, became tolerated in the next generation. What was tolerated then became accepted. What was accepted eventually became supported by many in the Body of Christ. What was then supported is now becoming law.

> "Because the sentence against an evil work is not executed speedily, therefore the heart of the sons of men is fully set in them to do evil." (Ecclesiastes 8:11)

God, as our Creator, intentionally designed the male and female relationship. He authored this dynamic connection in the beginning. Therefore, as the Author of the Book, He owns the copyright on relationship design. Since He owns the copyright He is the only One that can define it. Consider and understand that God has yet to assign us the authority to change this nor has He released legal permission to alter His quotes on the Book concerning gender and romance.

I am not speaking to the world here but to believers. Many heterosexual Christians are now affirming same sex relationships. To do so, however, is to separate what God has joined. It also misrepresents the Lord's heart and skews His nature in the eyes of unbelievers. We are doing the world no favors by affirming what God does not. When we support what God does not support, we put false words in God's mouth and thereby mischaracterize Him to the world.

How can we be the salt of the earth if we dismiss and invalidate the Word of God in order to please man and cooperate with the shifting times? How can we be an effective light in this world and yet also send a mixed and confusing signal through a compromising stand on biblical morality? The world deserves for the church to be all that Christ our Head calls us to be, especially when it concerns tough and challenging issues. God would rather we be cold or hot. I think the world feels the same way about us, too. Jesus is the most attractive person in the world. We don't need to change His words to get people to like Him. Remember, His name is 'Wonderful!' (Isaiah 9:6). If we can cooperate with the Holy Spirit to exalt the Prince of Peace, *He will draw* all men to Himself!

I believe that God is making a holy adjustment in our thinking. He's teaching us what it really means to be salt and light and true to the accuracy of the Holy Scriptures. He will help us to be and do just that without being self-righteous Pharisees or watered down believers.

> *Paul calls Christians the "Household of God, the church of the living God, the pillar and stay (the prop and support) of the Truth." (1 Timothy 3:15, AMP)*

Anyways, I don't mean to sound overly political here; but just realize that you are surrounded by a stronger same-sex influence than ever before. It is a force to be dealt with and you're right in the middle of it. We talked together in chapter eight about how the world, the flesh and the devil do not afford us the luxury of living idle spiritually. Most certainly, this intensified sexualized culture with its strong riptide doesn't allow you to be idle either.

The Safety of the Scriptures

That's one of the reasons it's so very important to be clear in the presentation of Biblical truth and to communicate the gospel as it is written and especially with the Father's heart: Same-sex activity will not liberate you by any means or free your inner person. One reason sin, including same-sex experimentation, creates confusion is that the more you act on the impulses of the lower nature (which is attached to you), the more you are identifying with it. The enemy will then lie to you and try to get you to believe that the flesh nature is who you really are and attempt to establish you in that false identity.

If you go down that path and persist in fleshly conduct, then the things of the "sensual" world will begin to make more "sense" to you. Homosexuality won't seem as wrong, or at least not a big deal to God, in your eyes. After violating God's loving boundaries, Adam and Eve's eyes were "opened." Yes, they were illuminated to a new world, but in a dark and binding way. Their eyes were opened but their new vision brought fear and death.

God, by the Tree of Life (His Word) and His Holy Spirit of Illumination can open your eyes, too. Thankfully, God's way produces true life and opens up the real you (Ephesians 1).

It is clear in Scripture that homosexuality violates God's design. Let's give the Creator a hearing:

> *"Do not practice homosexuality...It is a detestable sin."* (Leviticus 18:22, NLT)

> *"[Mankind] did vile and degrading things with each other's bodies. They traded the truth about God for a lie...Even the women turned against the natural way to have sex and instead indulged in sex with each other. And the men, instead of having normal sexual relations with women...did shameful things with other men, and as a result of this sin, they suffered within themselves the penalty they deserved."* (Romans 1:24-27, NLT)

Furthermore, in speaking of the call to stay away from all forms of sexual immorality, including homosexuality, the apostle Paul says, *"He who rejects this is not rejecting man but the God who gives His Holy Spirit to you"* (1 Thessalonians 4:8, NASB). These are sobering words of truth considering the conflicting opinions of society, and unfortunately, even among some in the Body of Christ today.

Although you may be experiencing some intense struggles concerning same-sex attraction, at least it can help to know that the Scriptures are clear about it. We are in a very confused, disoriented, vague and unstable world. We desperately need the comfort and safety of the Holy Scriptures. This is one of the many reasons why the gospel is still good news! It's a rock and an anchor to the soul. The Bible is God's immutable sworn oath to man, reliable, written in Blood, and is the end of all disputes (Hebrews 6:16). The Scriptures are the fountainhead of all truth, our plumb line, measuring rod, level, standard and our "more sure word of prophecy" (2 Peter 1:19, KJV). His Word is forever settled for us smack in the middle of this unsettling culture.

Don't make the mistake of "following your heart" if your heart goes against the grain of the Bible. Apart from the wisdom of God, our hearts have the capacity to be deceived and grow corrupt in no time at all (Jeremiah 17:9). God forbid we ever yield to pride and trust in our own experiences, assumptions, conclusions and perspective about life and God. The most noble sense of ideals and values can grow twisted real fast if they are not founded and rooted in the eternal. We all need a basis for what we believe that goes far beyond ourselves and our limited knowledge. We all need the compass of the Scriptures to guide us accurately; the anchor of the Word to keep us grounded; the plumb line of the commandments to keep us true; the mirror of the Bible to keep us in check.

Without the steadfast Word of God planted in our hearts, the result would be what we have today, *"everyone doing what is right in his own eyes"* (Judges 17:6). Some Americans like to call this way of thinking the "American spirit." In truth, this way of thinking is simply the prince of this world invading society with a spirit of self-rule, anti-Christ and rebellion. This is nothing new. Man fell to this in the garden as a married couple and we see it again now on a grand, world scale. Mankind is once again trying to build a prideful tower up to heaven in an effort to live independently of God. No problem. It will topple upon itself just like it did to the tower of Babel. Besides, we already know there is no one better to rule us than King Jesus.

> *"The kingdoms of this world have become the kingdoms of our Lord and of His Christ, and He shall reign forever and ever!"* (Revelation 11:15)

He also made us to be kings and priests to our God and to reign on earth with him (Revelation 5:10). Our King has already promised us joint authority and rulership in His superior Kingdom without all of the bondage attached to the deceiver's offer. The enemy is trying to sell us on being a god unto ourselves when God has already offered His plan to us first. This liar is up to his old tricks in the same way he suckered Adam. I encourage you then, instead of ruling and reigning yourself through selfishness, go ahead and rule and reign in Him and take dominion over self, principalities and powers! Crush the serpent's head just like your risen King did! He's got nothing you need.

In addition, don't let this present evil age put words in your mouth, thoughts in your brain and its seed in your heart. It wants to brainwash and persuade you of a lie that you're better off to rule yourself than to be ruled by a harsh and distant God. Yeah right! The world doesn't even know the real you or the Greater One that indwells you! The world needs what *you* have, not the other way around. Therefore, together now, we crush that high thought of self-rule and welcome the fire of the Holy Spirit to completely consume that altar of false worship right now, in Jesus mighty name!

So let's forget the so-called "American spirit." If it equals self-rule, we'd rather have the Holy Spirit than the American spirit! We choose the Tree of Life and the Perfect Law of Liberty, thank you very much! Give God some holy props for this. I know you agree.

Same-Sex Attractions

Same-sex attractions are legitimate. This reality is becoming much more common in the lives of many good young people. There's no sense trying to act like this issue is not real. This counseling of "quit it and forget it" isn't going to cut it either. If you are currently facing a challenge concerning same-sex attractions, I want to encourage you, with God's help, concerning His will for you:

1. You are not in sin for experiencing same-sex attractions: I know you want to honor God and please Him. Perhaps you desire to be free from these attractions. If that's you, He desires your freedom right along with you. One of my first prayers is that you would overcome any shame from this struggle. God is not ashamed of you or embarrassed about the challenge you're facing. You're not filthy for what you're dealing with. Shame will try to keep you bogged down and steal your courage to even reach out to God or others for help. Breakthrough from any shame you might be facing puts you on a level playing field to battle for your soon-coming victory. Although same-sex activity is outside of God's intent, your challenge against these impulses is common to many and is found in the Scriptures. God is for you. You'll need this encouragement for the battle ahead.

> *"For He has not despised nor abhorred the affliction of the afflicted; Nor has He hidden His face from Him; But when he cried to Him, He heard."* (Psalm 22:24)

2. You are not your feelings: Your emotions and affections do not define who you are. Every single one of us will experience, at different times, a number of various feelings, desires and passions. Thank God these impulses, although very legitimate, do not dictate our identity. The present culture would say that if you have feelings of same-sex attraction then you are probably gay. However, same-sex desires do not equal homosexuality. Furthermore, a person may in fact have been born with an orientation towards same-sex desires. However, their identity is not found in those driving urges. A generational bend towards illegal desires are very real. Again, as we discussed in chapter five, generational high places and strongholds are a reality. It is then helpful to remember that we were all born with some propensity to various passions. Again, the sin nature was an inherited human condition. Yet, simply because the lower nature had seemingly unbridled impulses (including the works of the flesh) does not mean that is who we are. Society may attempt to define identity by desires and feelings, but God doesn't. Misguided passions do not determine the limits of who you really are. You are who God says you are in Christ Jesus. We all have

CHAPTER 13

issues. We are His work-in-progress and a new creation, at the same time! You are not your affections.

> *"I will be glad and rejoice in Your mercy, for You have considered my trouble; You have known my soul in adversities, and have not shut me up into the hand of the enemy; You have set my feet in a wide place."* (Psalm 30:7-8)

3. You can resist same-sex impulses: Since we now see that God defines our identity, we can also appreciate this truth: our orientation toward a particular sin does not legitimize it. We understand that if mere desires should shape our conduct in society, then racism, rape and murder are justifiable since people deal with these driving desires and impulsive behaviors. If you're challenged with gay affections, you're not being dishonest for acknowledging them, nor are you dishonest for not giving in to them. Jesus doesn't ask us to pretend that we don't have problems or that these feelings do not exist. However, the essence of our walk with Christ involves denial (Matthew 16:24). Just because we were born with an inclination toward theft, substance abuse, gluttony or homosexuality, doesn't mean we have to act on these impulses or live that way. Neither does it make yielding to this conduct right. Jesus simply calls us to bring our problems and unhealthy patterns of behavior into His light through repentance. The Holy Spirit gives us the power to deny sinful desires. This quality of self-control is a fruit of the Spirit (Galatians 5:22-23).

> *"The temptations in your life are no different from what others experience. And God is faithful. He will not allow the temptation to be more than you can stand. When you are tempted, he will show you a way out so that you can endure."* (1 Corinthians 10:13, NLT)

4. There is forgiveness, healing, redemption and transformation through Christ: If you struggle with same-sex desires and would like God's help to follow a biblical pattern for wholeness, come to God just as you are. God doesn't expect you to straighten out your desires or overcome your tendencies first. I don't know how any of us wins this battle against the flesh apart from the

191

creative work of the Holy Spirit. He's the Great Transformer. You can be healed of your sexual pain, whether others inflicted it upon you, or you brought it on yourself. By His grace and with some help from trusted and qualified people, you can overcome whatever destructive desires and habits that have been robbing you of real life. It will take time and support but you can overcome it with God's help. You can be free from sin's mastery over you.

> *"For all have sinned and fall short of the glory of God."* (Romans 3:23)

Beyond any doubt, there is much more that should, can and has been written about same-sex affections. The resources are rich, vast and readily available to help people who are seeking freedom over their homosexual impulses and behaviors. Most importantly, true and lasting transformation for every single human includes seeing God for who He really is.

Experiencing the Father's Heart

As I write this chapter I sense how much He loves you. God doesn't feel that way about you because He sees you as a pathetic and helpless worm. You came from God and were in His heart before the foundations of the world. You are His very heart. You are his son, his daughter. It hurts me to see the enemy vigorously attempt to twist the nature of God in your eyes. God is not disgusted by your trial. He is not inconvenienced by your situation.

The Father's decision to be separated from His Son; the Son's willingness to obey the Father to do the same; the Lamb's intense suffering as He wouldn't even speak a word to save His life in order to save ours; all of it demonstrates God's unending commitment to love you and me, to deliver you and me. I pray the Lord, Your Creator, would show you in a real, most profound and convincing way His great love for you.

In this following passage, I believe, God is now speaking to you personally concerning your present struggle. It is a great and fiery trial for many of you. It is a fight for the healing of your heart; one for your contribution to your generation; one for your happiness; one for your very life. God weeps not only for you, but also with you. You are not alone. He is zealous about your deliverance. His response to your cry is swift! This passage tells how David cried out to God for rescue from life threatening danger and then shows God's awesome response for his son.

> "The pangs of death surrounded me, and the floods of ungodliness made me afraid. The sorrows of Sheol surrounded me; The snares of death confronted me. In my distress I called upon the Lord, and cried out to my God; **He heard my voice** from His temple, and **my cry came before Him,** even to His ears. **Then** the earth shook and trembled; The foundations of the hills also quaked and were shaken, because He was angry. Smoke went up from His nostrils, and devouring fire from His mouth; Coals were kindled by it. He bowed the heavens also, and came down with darkness under His feet. And He rode upon a cherub, and flew; He flew upon the wings of the wind. He made darkness His secret place; His canopy around Him was dark waters and thick clouds of the skies. From the brightness before Him, His thick clouds passed with hailstones and coals of fire. **The Lord thundered from heaven, and the Most High uttered His voice, hailstones and coals of fire. He sent out His arrows and scattered the foe, lightnings in abundance, and He vanquished them. Then the channels of the sea were seen, the foundations of the world were uncovered at Your rebuke, O Lord, at the blast of the breath of Your nostrils. He sent from above, He took me; He drew me out of many waters. He delivered me from my strong enemy, from those who hated me, for they were too strong for me.** They confronted me in the day of my calamity, but the Lord was my support. He also brought me out into a broad place; **He delivered me because He delighted in me.**" (Psalms 18:4-19 NKJV)

God did all of this for His son, David. God's response to David's cry was amazing. I believe He's doing the same for you now.

In Conclusion

In all of this, I pray for your God and Father to reveal His heart to you and for you. Jesus truly is the way, the truth and the life. He desires you find life in Him, and enjoy it fully. Part of God's pattern for your life is sex as He intended. This blueprint is found only in His life-giving Word. Although this chapter adds another dimension to this book, it was necessary.

You're in a world that lies under the sway of the wicked one. There is more at stake for you than just marrying the person God has for you. The world, the flesh and the devil are seeking to confuse your very identity, steal your purpose and rob you of life. Yet, although it may not seem like it, you are not the underdog. Call on God right now and let's see Him respond in a powerful way.

> *"Call to Me and I will answer and show you great and mighty things, fenced in and hidden, which you do not know (do not distinguish and recognize, have knowledge of and understand."* (Jeremiah 33:3, AMP)

Align yourself completely with Jesus. Be great in your generation and for your generation. Remember, you're not like everybody else. Love you.

PRAYER:

Almighty God, You are Creator and Lord. Your Word is the fountainhead of all truth. Your way is best and is only for my good. With all of my heart I desire to align myself with Your design for sex and life. I receive Your grace and wisdom to pursue the heterosexual marriage you have planned for me. Deliver me from the spirit of this age. I want nothing to do with it. Lord Jesus, I repent of experimenting sexually. I want to be delivered and transformed from any and all forms of same sex attractions. I receive the cleansing power of the blood of Christ to sanctify me. In Jesus name I also cast off the filth, shame, darkness, lies and confusion that have been tormenting my life. If I stumble into sin later today, I will repent and get back up. If I am to forgive others 490 times in one day, for sure You will forgive me, love me and pick me up again at least the same amount! With Your help Lord, I will no longer wander in sexual confusion. I ask for Your Holy Spirit to fill me in a fresh and powerful way. I submit to You Father, and I resist the devil and all His lies concerning my sexual desires and my sexual identity. I ask that You unleash the real me! Make me a light for Christ in this dark world and use me to lead many into His saving knowledge. I pray that you direct me into right relationships that will support Your work in my life. In Your name Lord Jesus, Amen.

PRAYER TO RECEIVE JESUS AS SAVIOR AND LORD:

Dear Lord, I am totally lost. I cannot figure out my life or the world I live in. I come to You asking that You rescue me. I believe in You. I don't understand everything I hope to, but I do believe You are who the Bible says You are. Jesus, I believe You came into the earth two thousand years ago. You came because God loved me and knew I needed saving. I believe You died on a cross and were resurrected on the third day. I ask you to enter into my heart and be my Lord. Forgive me of all my sins. I now receive the gift of eternal life. Thank you that I'm now going to heaven and my name is written in the Book of Life. Please bring the right people into my life and direct my steps into Your will for me. Fill me with Your Holy Spirit. Please give me a hunger to read the Bible. Place me into Your family through a local church of Your choosing. Thank you for saving me! In Christ's name I pray, Amen (Romans 10:9-10, Revelation 21:27, John 3:16-18, John 20:30-31).

Congratulations! If you prayed that prayer, writing this whole book was worth it! I'd love it if you emailed us at email@reachingforwardmedia.com and leave a message saying, "I prayed the prayer!" God bless, champion. You're awesome.

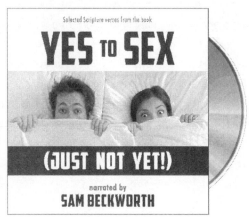
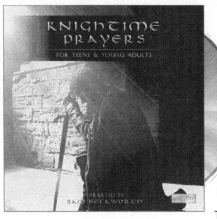

Notes

CHAPTER 1

1. By permission. From *Merriam-Webster's Collegiate® Dictionary*, Eleventh Edition. Copyright © 2012 by Merriam-Webster, Incorporated. www.Merriam-Webster.com.

CHAPTER 2

1. Gladiator, dir. by Ridley Scott (2000; Columbia TriStar, 2000 dvd).

2. From *Every Young Man's Battle*, by Fred Stoeker and Steven Arterburn with Mike Yorkey. Copyright © 2002 by Steven Arterburn, Fred Stoeker, and Mike Yorkey. Used by permission of WaterBrook Multnomah, an Imprint of the Crown Publishing Group, a division of Random House, Inc. Any third party use of this material, outside of this publication, is prohibited. Interested parties must apply directly to Random House, Inc. for permission.

CHAPTER 4

1. Taken from *Relationships,* by Dr.'s Les and Leslie Parrott. Copyright © 1998 by Les and Leslie Parrott. Use by permission of Zondervan. www.zondervan.com.

2. By permission. From *Merriam-Webster's Collegiate® Dictionary*, Eleventh Edition. Copyright © 2012 by Merriam-Webster, Incorporated www.Merriam-Webster.com.

3. Fatal Attractions, by Jack Hayford, p. 12. Copyright © 2004. Gospel Light/ Regal Books, Ventura, CA 93003. Used by permission.

CHAPTER 5

1. Reprinted by permission. *Who Switched Off My Brain*, by Dr. Caroline Leaf. Copyright © 2009. Thomas Nelson Inc. Nashville, Tennessee. All rights reserved.

2. Reprinted by permission. *Who Switched Off My Brain*, by Dr. Caroline Leaf. Copyright © 2009. Thomas Nelson Inc. Nashville, Tennessee. All rights reserved.

3. Taken from Boundaries, by Dr. Henry Cloud and Dr. John Townsend. Copyright © 1992 by Henry Cloud and John Townsend. Use by permission of Zondervan. www.zondervan.com.

CHAPTER 6

1. Who I Am in Christ, by Neil T. Anderson, p. 110. Copyright © 2002. Gospel Light/Regal Books, Ventura, CA 93003. Used by permission.

CHAPTER 7

1. Uncle Buck, dir. by John Hughes (1989; Universal Home Entertainment, 1998 dvd).

CHAPTER 8

1. The Lord of the Rings: The Two Towers, dir. by Peter Jackson (2002; New Line Home Video, 2003 dvd).

2. Art of War: Public Domain.

3. Strong's Exhaustive Concordance. Public Domain.

4. Strong's Exhaustive Concordance. Public Domain.

5. Reprinted by permission. *Kissed the Girls and Made Them Cry*,
by Lisa Bevere. Copyright © 2002. Thomas Nelson Inc. Nashville, Tennessee.
All rights reserved.

6. *Strong's Exhaustive Concordance*. Public Domain.

CHAPTER 9

1. *City Slickers,* dir. by Ron Underwood (1991; Mgm, 2002 dvd).

2. By permission. From *Merriam-Webster's Collegiate® Dictionary*,
Eleventh Edition. Copyright © 2012 by Merriam-Webster, Incorporated.
www.Merriam-Webster.com.

2. *The Right Guy for the Right Girl*, by Debby Jones and Jackie Kendall.
Copyright © 2010 by Debby Jones and Jackie Kendall. Reproduced by
permission of Destiny Image Publishers.

CHAPTER 10

1. Excerpt from *Odd Girl Out: The Hidden Culture of Aggression in Girls*,
by Rachel Simmons. Copyright © 2002 by Rachel Simmons.
Reprinted by permission of Houghton Mifflin Harcourt
Publishing Company. All rights reserved.

2. Taken from *Your Knight in Shining Armor.* Copyright © 1995
by P.B. Wilson. Published by Harvest House Publisher Eugene,
Oregon 97402. www.harvesthousepublishers.com.
Used by Permission.

3. Strong's Exhaustive Concordance. Public Domain.

4. Taken from *Sacred Singleness.* Copyright © 2009 by
Winston and Brooks, Inc. Published by Harvest House Publishers
Eugene, Oregon 97402. www.harvesthousepublishers.com.
Used by Permission.

CPSIA information can be obtained at www.ICGtesting.com
Printed in the USA
BVOW02s1200280416

445988BV00015B/74/P